LAST MINUTE

Retirement Planning

By
Stephen M. Rosenberg, CFP

CAREER PRESS

Franklin Lakes, NJ

LAST MINUTE RETIREMENT PLANNING

Cover design by Foster & Foster

Printed in the U.S.A. by Book-mart Press

To order this title, please call toll-free 1-800-CAREER-1 (NJ and Canada: 201-848-0310) to order using VISA or MasterCard, or for further information on books from Career Press.

The Career Press, Inc., 3 Tice Road, PO Box 687, Franklin Lakes, NJ 07417

Library of Congress Cataloging-in-Publication Data

Rosenberg, Stephen M., 1944-
    Last minute retirement planning / by Stephen M. Rosenberg, CFP.
        p.   cm.
    Includes index.
    ISBN 1-56414-376-7 (pbk.)
        1. Retirement income--Planning.   I. Title.
    HG179.R684   1999
    332.024'01--dc21   98-34860

Dedication

This book is dedicated to my children, David, Jeffrey, Laura, and Stephanie. May the information shared in this book serve you as well as it has served me.

Contents

Part II: Your Secure Retirement

Part I

Securing Your Retirement Dreams

Chapter 1

Your journey to retirement security starts here

Retirement. Has a nice ring, doesn't it? It's the time we all live for: when we get to walk out the door and not have to work anymore. Relaxation. Travel. Time with your family. A long vacation at the beach. Weeks on end in your vacation cottage in the mountains. Touring North America in your motor home. Your dream cruise to Alaska.

Hold it! For most Americans, that comfortable retirement is merely a dream. The reality of retirement is spending your last years unable to do the things you want to do for lack of money. It's a retirement full of worry and concern: Will I be able to pay my bills? What if I get sick? What happens if I go into a nursing home? What if my children need help? What if I need repairs to my home?

It's sad but true: By the age of 65, most people are either dead or dead broke. In fact, government statistics show that out of 100 people reaching the age of 65, only two are financially independent. The rest must either depend on relatives, the federal government, or must continue working in order to survive.

But let's forget the negative statements and face one glorious fact: You can make your retirement as wonderful as you want. It only requires that you make smart decisions with your money.

As an investment advisor to hundreds of retirees, I know exactly what it takes to secure the retirement of your dreams. But even though I'm going to tell you what you need to do, I can't make you do it. I can only guide you and urge you. As the saying goes, "You can lead a horse to water but you can't make it drink." I can tell you all the right things to do. But ultimately, when my back is turned, you have the right to do something stupid! And that's what will mess you up.

If you've got a while until retirement

I started out writing this book for people facing imminent retirement. But as I got deeper into it, I realized that a tremendous benefit can be enjoyed by people still far from retirement, simply because they have more options to achieve financial security. If this describes you, it's nice to know that those extra years can give you two advantages: First, you can afford to make some mistakes along the way because you have the time to correct them—or at least learn what not to do; and second, you have more time for your good decisions to work for you. Therefore, consider yourself fortunate. Most people wait until it's too late to do any retirement planning—thus the title of this book. If you are young, I congratulate you on your desire to achieve retirement security. But desire is only one part of the puzzle—the easy part. The tough part is following through. I will help you do just that.

If you're retiring tomorrow

Even if you are right around the corner from retirement, this book will help you tremendously. Why? Because most people's goal is to retire at 55. Statistically, if you are married and you and your spouse are both 55, one of you will live to age 90. That's 35 years longer! Therefore, even if you are retiring tomorrow, it's still vital that you make the proper choices to allow you to live comfortably another 30 or 35 years.

A scary thought

Let me give you another fact that I hope will scare you into making good decisions. The average person starts working after finishing high school or college. Let's say for the sake of argument that you begin your career at age 22. Let's also say that the average retirement age is 57. That's 35 years of work. Now, as I said before, you have a good probability of being retired for another 35 years. But there's a big difference between the 35 years you are working and the 35 years you are not. During the first 35 years, your income increases over the years. You get raises. You get promotions. You are able to invest money for your retirement.

But once you're retired, all that changes. No more raises. No more promotions. But the cost of living continues to go up. And you still have another 35 years! That should give you an idea of what you are facing in the years ahead. I hope, too, it will emphasize your need to plan properly, whether you're 30 years from retiring, or 30 minutes.

The information I am providing has been derived from two sources: my own financial situation, and those of the people I have counseled and taught over the years. I hold the degree of Certified Financial Planner (CFP). I have been in the financial industry since the early 1970s, so I'm not a young "Johnny come lately" who is relatively new in the investment business and yet still thinks he "knows it all." My college degrees are great, but I've received the best degree from what a friend of mind calls UHK—The University of Hard Knocks.

I've been president of my own investment advisory firm since the late 1980s. I've written best-selling financial books. I have been quoted in top newspapers and financial magazines in the country. I have appeared on radio and television from coast to coast in addition to having my own financial call-in show. I have taught graduate-level financial courses for a major university. I share my knowledge with the world through books like this. And I present pre-retirement seminars for Fortune 500 companies.

I've been there

But more than that, I've been there. It wasn't always glory for me. I faced the hardship of a financially disastrous divorce. My present wife, Nancy, was a widow who raised her two young children only on the income she derived from her two jobs. She received no life insurance when her husband died. No family help, no government assistance, nothing. Through the years, we have enjoyed the financial highs and suffered through the lows. We have faced the normal problems of raising and educating children, taking care of older relatives, etc. We've had ups and downs just like you. Together, Nancy and I started from ground zero (actually less than zero) and built our retirement security. We did it by following the principles you will learn in Part I of this book. So I'm not asking you to do anything I haven't done. Rather, I'm giving you "street smart" knowledge that will help you achieve your retirement dreams.

A unique perspective

My financial experience, plus that of my clients, gives me a unique "before and after" perspective on retirement.

Although I haven't experienced my own retirement yet, I live it daily through my clients. I enjoy the time I spend with them, because for the most part, they are enjoying the fruits of their labors. Understand that my clients are not your average man or woman on the street. They are, for the most part, financially secure. They worked hard, they saved, and they invested their money wisely.

Financially, my clients are more successful than the general population. That's because I limit my practice to people with at least $100,000 to invest. My average fee-based account size is more than $500,000.

I tell you this not to brag, but for two reasons. First, I learned long ago that you move forward only by listening to successful people. When I give my clients advice, they are getting it from someone who, like most of them, has come from nothing to something. I made mistakes, but I did a whole lot more right. And that's why I am where I am today.

The second reason I tell you this is because you might want to work with a financial advisor. It is important that you work with someone who is successful himself or herself and who also works with prosperous clients. You want someone who specializes in working with retirees and pre-retirees, as I do.

Not your typical author

Unlike most financial authors, I'm on the financial front lines every day. I'm not a professional writer; I'm a professional advisor. I see people like you every day. I talk to people like you on my radio show every week. And I meet people like you at my seminars and corporate programs.

And, like you, I have to provide for my own retirement. I can't depend on rich relatives or an inheritance to bring me security. My wife and I put money each and every month into our retirement plans, just like I tell my working clients to do.

So let's get on with it. In this first part of the book, I will cover those aspects of finance that are relevant to everyone. In the second part, I will give you a basic guideline that you can use to determine, depending on where you are in your life, where you should be financially. I don't know if you're 30 years old with 30 years to go, or 60 years old and retiring the day after tomorrow. But in any case, hopefully you will have a long life still ahead of you, and you deserve to make those years the best they can be. The information that follows will help you achieve your retirement dreams.

Chapter 2

Your vision: Everything happens twice

Why am I writing this book? For a very simple reason. I have a vision for my professional life. Some might call it a mission statement: to have a positive impact on the lives of others so they can enjoy a secure, happy retirement.

Now, I know I can't meet with everyone who wants to see me personally. As I told you in the introduction, I have to limit the scope of my practice. But that doesn't mean I can't achieve my vision. I can, and I do it not only through writing this book, but through my teaching as well as my radio and television appearances. Everything I do from a business standpoint gets me closer to my vision.

In addition, I have a vision as to what I want to achieve financially. And my wife I have our vision of what we want our personal and family relationships to be. All this sounds nice, but it has a real message: We make sure that everything we do gets us closer to achieving our vision.

Achieving your vision

Having a vision enables you to spend most of your time doing only those activities that will get you closer to where you want to be. In other words, you will stay on track.

When I meet potential clients who are getting ready to retire, I see a noticeable difference between those who have planned for the future and those who have just gone along hoping for the best. And that distinction manifests itself in several forms. Primarily, it's an optimism for the future, a more comfortable life style, and a warm feeling that they have made good decisions.

I am currently working with a very good client who has a charitable idea that he is trying to bring to fruition. Every time we talk about it, he says that he has in his mind what he wants, he just needs help and guidance to carry it out. That's exactly what I'm talking about. You get a vision in your mind, you keep focusing on it, and it eventually happens. It's amazing! Just like magic.

Too many regrets

Unfortunately, most people don't get to realize the benefit of good choices. Instead, they look back and see wasted opportunities and bad decisions. That's because they didn't have a clear idea of what they wanted. They were continually wobbling in different directions.

In my meetings with retirees and pre-retirees, I hear three primary regrets:

1. I should have saved more for retirement.
2. I shouldn't have taken money out of my retirement accounts while I was still working.
3. I should have invested my money more wisely.

Lack of vision

All three of these regrets are the result of a lack of vision. These people were so caught up in their day-to-day living that they didn't really plan for their retirement.

After all, they had good reasons (or so they thought) not to worry about retirement:

- I've got a family to raise and that takes money.
- I have to worry about my children's education.
- I want to enjoy myself while I'm young.
- I want my kids to have what I never had.
- The Smiths have a new car, why shouldn't we?
- What happens if I put things off, and I don't live long enough to enjoy retirement?
- Why should I accumulate all this money just for my kids to waste?
- The government is going to get it anyway; I might as well spend it now.

Out of control

This type of thinking is typical. I call it "life out of control." You are like a twig floating down a stream: You let life take you wherever it might and you make rash, arbitrary decisions because they sound good or they are easy.

But I want you to remember something: Nobody becomes financially secure by accident. You read about successful people—they all had goals; they all had visions. They all knew what they wanted to accomplish.

When I meet with people who want me to be their financial advisor, what I need to know first and foremost are their goals. How can I ever hope to help people who don't know what they want to accomplish? If they don't know what they want, how am I supposed to know?

Trade-offs

Remember one thing about life: It's full of trade-offs. You exchange one action for one result. Throughout your life, you make all kinds of choices, both good and bad. The interesting thing is that the people who make good financial choices end up with a lot more money than the people who make bad financial choices.

Now, I know that sounds obvious, but let me ask you a question. If it is so obvious that good choices lead to better results, then why do so many people make bad choices? Is it because they are stupid? I don't think so. It's all because of 1) a lack of training and the resulting fear of handling and investing their money; 2) not understanding how money can work for them; and 3) focusing on the wrong thing.

If you take the time to read, highlight, and understand what I am telling you, you will go a long way to taking care of numbers one and two. The big thing, however, is where you go with that knowledge. And that brings us to number three: focus.

Focusing

A huge key to your financial success is controlling your focus. By focus I mean that you can either concentrate on that which leads you to make stupid financial decisions (buying stuff you don't need, wasting money, etc.), or you can concentrate on the benefits of making smart decisions (peace of mind, secure retirement, etc.) And, by the way, I'm not saying you're stupid if you make stupid decisions. I am using the word "stupid" to emphasize what most bad decisions really turn out to be when you look back on them.

According to Tony Robbins, a peak performance coach, everything we do is to avoid pain or to achieve pleasure. And given a choice between the two, most people do anything to avoid pain, even if it means giving up the benefits that achieving pleasure would bring.

For example, you want to go on a diet. Instead of focusing on how great you're going to feel and look when you lose the weight, instead of focusing on the better quality of life you're going to enjoy, you focus on the pain of doing without the chocolate eclairs and candy bars. In other words, you associate pleasure with eating and pain with not eating. And until your pain outweighs your pleasure, you won't change.

Focusing on the wrong thing

The same thing is true with money. You can either focus on the pain and misery of "doing without," or you can focus on the pleasure of knowing that you are making wise financial decisions that will benefit you in the long run. The choice is up to you.

I think one of the reasons my wife and I have been so successful financially is that we feel pleasure when we invest and spend our money wisely, and we feel pain when we spend it foolishly. My favorite check I write each month is my contribution to my retirement plan. Now, that's not to say we don't sometimes waste money and that we don't sometimes make stupid decisions, because we do. But it's very rare. We have achieved our financial success because we have been very careful with our money for the 10 years we've been married. We continue to put money into our retirement plans first, making sure our retirement years are secure, before we spend money on "stuff."

Spend it now?

The phrase I hear a lot is, "Why shouldn't we be able to enjoy ourselves while we're young? After all, we might not even live until retirement, and then all the money we've saved will be wasted."

That sounds logical, but that thinking is counter-productive. In fact, it guarantees that you won't have enough for retirement.

Yes, you could die tomorrow. But statistically, that's not going to happen. The reality is that you'll probably live awhile, and likely experience a long retirement. So your biggest risk isn't that you'll die too soon, it's that you'll live too long.

So it's a trade-off. You can rationalize spending money today all you want. But unless you plan for the future, you'll be pretty miserable for two reasons. First, you'll spend your time today worrying about how you are going to support your lavish life style. And second, you'll spend your retirement years regretting the missed opportunities and bad decisions you made when you were young. In other words, you will be unhappy both today and in retirement.

Being frugal is the key

Don't take my word for it. Take a look around you. The financially successful people who enjoy an abundant retirement today tend to be those who were careful with their money yesterday. In *The Millionaire Next Door* by Thomas Stanley, Ph.D., and William Danko, Ph.D., the authors explain what they learned after studying average people who became millionaires. I'm not talking about the Donald Trump/Ted Turner type of millionaire. I'm talking about the you and me type of millionaire: average people who made smart decisions with their money and accumulated more than a million dollars. Do you know the primary reason they were so financially successful? Not because they were given money by their parents or won the lottery. Not because they were in the right place at the right time. It was because they were frugal in their spending habits. Not cheap. Not stingy. Not miserly. Frugal. And take it from someone who chooses to be frugal: You can still enjoy a great, fulfilling life.

But you won't accumulate wealth by focusing on how deprived you are because you don't choose to drive a BMW. You can't do it by being jealous because your friends are taking a cruise every year and you choose not to. You can't do it by feeling sorry for yourself if you don't choose to live in a big house, or feeling sorry for your kids because all their friends are wearing designer jeans and you choose to spend your money more meaningfully.

Your choice

This brings us to my favorite word: choose. For years, I have driven my kids crazy with this, and today I do the same to everyone else. Well, I'm not going to let you off the hook, either!

Notice in the previous section I said "choose" to spend money on certain items. As far as I know, nobody has ever held a gun to anyone's head to made them buy a Lexus, or wear Tommy Hilfiger jackets, or wear $150 Nike sneakers. These are all choices. And until you realize that everything you do is because you choose to do it, then you will be at the mercy of everyone else, and you'll be that twig floating wherever the stream takes you.

And by the way, what happens when a storm (financial emergency) hits? That twig is washed ashore, so when the water withdraws, it withers up and dies. Sound like anyone you know?

It's really a question of choices. As a nation, we have become a bunch of blamers. No one wants to accept responsibility for their own actions; they want to blame someone else. So it goes with money. "It's not my fault I don't have money to pay my bills." And on it goes.

It's about time you take control of your life and realize that you choose how you spend your money.

As we move forward through this book, think of ways you can choose to change your habits. Think about what you would do if you could...and then do it! It's really easier than you think. It just takes courage on your part.

One final thought

Or maybe two! Investing requires planning—long-term planning. Creating retirement security is a marathon, not a 100-yard dash. Too many people are looking for a quick, easy solution to their financial problems. They look for hot stock tips and gimmicks. They listen to promoters who have a great scheme to get rich quick. Unfortunately, there is no such thing. Investing your money is like raising your children. It takes lots of patience and discipline.

Chapter 3

Debt: Satan or salvation?

One of the biggest stumbling blocks to your secure retirement is your debt. It's so easy to spend, spend, spend—or I should say charge, charge, charge! In fact, it is so easy that people end up in financial hell because of it.

Well, I don't want that to happen to you. So let's talk about what we can do to make sure that you control your debt, not the other way around.

Credit is a double-edged sword. It helps you buy items you need, but it also makes it too easy for you to get into financial trouble. Credit makes you more concerned with the monthly payment than with total cost. Just look at the way cars are sold. That's how you get into trouble—fast! Let's look at the aspects of credit and what you need to know.

Your home mortgage

You have three decisions to make when it comes to getting a home mortgage: the type of loan, the length of the loan, and the interest rate.

Type of mortgage

There are primarily two types of mortgages: fixed rate and adjustable rate.

Fixed rate mortgages provide a level interest rate throughout the term of the loan. If interest rates go up, you get the benefit of your lower-rate loan. On the other hand, if rates go down, you are stuck with that higher rate. Of course, you can always refinance to get a lower rate.

Adjustable rate mortgages, also known as ARMs, provide a variable rate based on current interest rates. If rates go up, your rate goes up, and vice versa. ARMs normally offer an appealingly low interest rate the first year, and adjust upward from there. ARMs contain annual and lifetime caps. The annual cap limits the amount a rate can increase or decrease each year; the lifetime cap does the same over the life of the mortgage.

One aspect of an ARM you need to understand is that the initial rate is a "teaser" rate—it is lower than it should be just to attract you. The actual rate of an ARM is calculated by adding a factor, usually 2.75 percent, to an index, usually the 12-month Treasury bill rate. Therefore, if you are offered a rate of 5 percent and the actual Treasury bill rate is 5 percent, then your rate should be 7.75 percent (the Treasury bill rate plus the 2.75 percent factor). So you know one thing for sure: Unless interest rates totally collapse, your rate (and thus your payment) is going to go up the next year, and probably the year after. Therefore, even if rates stay the same, the interest rate on the mortgage will adjust upward at the first anniversary.

Which one is right for you

Choosing the right type of mortgage is extremely difficult because it depends on future interest rates. The low payments of an ARM make them attractive. But if you buy your house on the basis of an artificially low interest rate, you are going to be unpleasantly shocked in the years ahead.

In my opinion, fixed rate mortgages offer big advantages, especially in this day of low mortgage rates, for several reasons:

- You know what your monthly payment will be and you can budget accordingly.

- You won't be shocked with increases in future years.

- If rates drop substantially, you can always refinance.

15-year vs. 30-year

If you want to make the most of your mortgage, my advice is to get rid of it as soon as possible! In other words, pay it off. You will have peace of mind, plus save thousands of dollars.

Now there are some who will argue with me. They will say that you should get the biggest mortgage you can and pay it off as slowly as possible. Then, take the difference in the payments and invest it in the stock market. While this might get you a better return over time, there is no guarantee.

But, remember, I work primarily with retirees. The fact is that most people, especially those getting nearer to retirement, like the security of having a paid-for home. That way, no matter what happens, they'll always have a place to live.

Credit cards

Credit cards are a major part of our life. You can't travel without one. You can't cash a check without one. You need them for everything. To help us poor slobs enjoy a better life, the credit card companies, out of the kindness of their hearts, have made it so easy for us to get credit. Aren't they sweet?

Now don't get me wrong, credit cards do have their place. But they possess enough danger to cause people incredible financial harm. Of course, credit cards can't create harm, only people can choose to create their own harm by misusing credit. So, before we start, let's lay the blame where it belongs: on the users, not the companies who make easy credit readily available.

Minimum payment

What happens to credit card holders is they get caught up in the "minimum payment" scam. Look at this example with a 16 percent credit card:

Credit balance	**$3,000**
Finance charge for the month	**$40**
Minimum payment	**$51**

You may not realize it, but if you pay the $51 minimum, only $11 goes toward reducing your balance. Think of how many months it will take to reduce a $3,000 balance at the rate of $11 per month. You may not live that long!

See why this is a scam? The credit card companies are collecting 15 to 21 percent on all those Americans who are only making minimum payments. No wonder they make so much money.

Reducing credit card costs

Here are a few ways you can reduce your credit card expenses:

1. **Don't use them.** This is the best solution, but not realistic for most people.

2. **Pay your balance in full every month.** Again, this is not always possible.

3. **Shop for the best interest rate.** Rates vary greatly on credit cards. If you are not going to pay your balance in full every month, then this is very important. Why pay 19 percent when you can pay 8 percent?

4. **Shop for lowest annual fee.** If you are not going to carry a balance, then get a card with no annual fee. If you pay your balance in full each month, then the interest rate doesn't matter.

Debt consolidation loans

Potentially the most expensive type of loan is a debt consolidation loan. Let's assume you have $15,000 in credit card and car loans and you're paying $595 per month. You're reading the paper one morning and you see an ad with this headline: "Borrow $10,000 for only $78.67 per month. Home equity loans—rates start at 8.75 percent." The schedule of loans and payments in the ad showed that you could consolidate your debts into a single $15,000 loan with a monthly payment of only $118.01 for 360 months. Sounds good, doesn't it? Well, it couldn't be worse. The following chart shows the true results.

	Number of Payments	Total Paid
Current Debt	30 months @ $595.00	$17,850
Consolidation	360 months @ $118.01	$42,483

If you choose the new loan, you will have to pay $42,483 over a 30-year period versus being out of debt in 30 months. The problem is that the ad looks so good: only 8.75 percent instead of the 15 to 18 percent you're currently paying. But you must look past the monthly payments and interest rate and consider the total payments. *Remember, you cannot borrow your way out of debt!*

Paying off your debt

A good goal is to get out of debt. In fact, you should make it your primary goal to be debt-free no later than the day you retire. So let's look at a few aspects of getting out of debt.

The best investment you can make

Do you want a safe, high-yield investment, with no risk of loss? Pay off your credit cards! If you have credit cards charging 18 percent and money in the bank earning 4 percent, why not take your money out of the bank and pay off your credit cards? That turns a 4 percent investment (before taxes) into an 18 percent investment (after taxes). What a deal!

If you can't pay off your credit cards totally, then at least pay more than the minimum. Anything above that will reduce your principal. As stated previously, paying just the minimum payment is a losing situation. How much of a losing situation?

According to Bankcard Holders of America, if you have a $2,500 balance on an 18.5 percent credit card, and you pay only the minimum balance monthly, *it will take more than 30 years to pay it off!* You will pay more than $6,600 in interest! Instead, make extra payments and get rid of that albatross.

Getting out of debt

Okay, you owe some money—in fact you owe lots of money. You realize the errors of your ways. You swear that once you get out of debt you will never run up your credit cards again. What do you do?

First, you've got to ask yourself if you're really serious. Has the pain reached a high enough level to motivate you to really go ahead with this? Do you realize that all the money you are paying in interest is jeopardizing your future security? Would you rather put the money in your own pocket instead of the credit card company? Then let's go for it.

There are several theories on how to reduce debt. Some people say to pay the highest interest rate first. Some say to pay the lowest balance first. I agree with the latter.

You need a systematized plan to pay off your debt. You need some successes. If you are going to get your debt paid over a five-year period, for example, then the interest rate you pay is not that relevant.

So here's what you do. Make a list of every debt you have, starting with the largest balance and working down to the smallest. Beside each creditor, list the minimum monthly payment. Divide the amount that you owe by the monthly payment. That will give you a figure which represents how long it will take you to pay off that loan at the current rate.

Then list them in order of the shortest period first. Finally, scrape up any additional money that you can pay above all the minimums, and put it all toward the first account. Once that one is paid in full, take all the money that you were paying toward that one, add it to what you're paying on the second, and pay that one off. And keep going until all are paid. That will give you some successes along the way that will motivate you to keep progressing.

Keep in mind that the use of credit should benefit *you*, not the credit card company. Your goal should be to be *out* of debt. Remember that their goal is to keep you *in* debt. They are not your friend. They are doing nothing to help you. They care only about themselves, and that can be very costly to you.

Chapter 4

Compound interest: Your greatest friend

If you're going to be financially successful, there is one theory you must understand. It is the one topic that will determine whether you develop retirement security. If you understand this concept, you will accumulate wealth; if you don't, you won't. If you see every investment you make, and every big purchase you consider, in light of this concept, the difference in accumulated wealth—and your ultimate security—will be mind-boggling.

When Albert Einstein was asked what he thought man's greatest discovery was, he responded, "The power of compounding." To reiterate, people who understand compounding make money; those who don't, don't.

Compound interest goes to work when your money makes money, and that money, left to accumulate, in turn makes even more money. You put $10,000 in a 5 percent certificate of deposit. At the end of the year, you will have $10,500. If you leave that entire $10,500 to accumulate, the next year you will make more than $500; you will make $525. Now that might not seem like a lot, but over time, it adds up.

More money

The magic of compound interest really shows up over long periods of time. That's why most people ignore it; they are short-term oriented. They only want to know what will help them today. Well, let's start off on the right foot. From now on, we're going to make decisions that make sense over time, not just today and tomorrow. In other words, we're not going to exchange short-term gratification for long-term disaster.

Let's assume you invest $100 per month for a period of 20 years and you earn 10 percent per year (don't worry about how you're going to earn 10 percent; I'll show you that later). Over the 20 years, you will have invested $24,000, but the value of your account will have grown to $75,937. That's compound interest. Let's assume you stop adding money, but you leave the $75,937 to continue to grow. In another 10 years, that account would be worth $196,961! All this from a measly $3.33 a day! That's really compound interest.

Assume you invest $6.67 a day, $200 per month, for 30 years. You will have invested $72,000, but the value of your account will have grown to $452,098. That is the value of letting compound interest work for you. If you had spent your interest every year, you would still only have $72,000; this way you have more than $450,000! That's quite a difference.

The rule of 72s

Now, it's nice to know that money is going to grow. But what's an easy way to determine how fast it's going to grow? By using something called the "rule of 72s." This lets you easily compute the approximate number of years it will take a sum of money to double.

To get the answer, divide 72 by the interest rate. The result is the approximate amount of time it will take your money to double. Here. I'll do it for you:

Your rate of return	How long it will take your money to double
3%	24 years
5%	14.4 years
7%	10.25 years
9%	8 years
10%	7.2 years
12%	6 years
15%	4.8 years
20%	3.6 years

Consequences

Your understanding of compound interest will allow you to make wise financial decisions because you'll recognize the consequences of your actions. Let me give you an example.

Clients of mine came into my office and were considering withdrawing $16,000 from their retirement plan to pay off some bills. The husband is 43, the wife is 41, and they want to retire in 21 years.

I told them before they make any decision, they need to consider the consequences of that decision. First, they needed to recognize that in order to be left with $16,000 after taxes, they would need to withdraw $30,000 from their retirement plan. That's because federal and state taxes, plus the 10 percent early distribution penalty, would take almost $14,000! Second, they had to recognize that the $30,000 would no longer be working for them. And third, they should recognize the financial consequences of the $30,000 no longer working for them.

My clients see the light

The first consequence shocked them. They didn't think they would lose almost 45 percent of the money to taxes. The second one was no big deal, because they knew they would not be earning anything on the money they withdrew. But the third factor blew them away. I'm going to show you what I showed them.

If they left the $30,000 in their plan, it would double every 7.2 years, based on an average 10 percent rate of return. Now understand that they were making much more than 10 percent, but that won't always be the case. So $30,000 could double three times between now and the day they retire. $30,000 turns into $60,000 in 7.2 years; $60,000 turns into $120,000 in another 7.2 years, and $120,000 turns into $240,000 in another 7.2 years.

Using our assumptions, it would cost them almost *a quarter of a million dollars* between now and the time they retire to get the benefit of $16,000 (after taxes) today. What would you do? Would you trade $240,000 at retirement for $16,000 today? I certainly hope not.

Higher rates *and* compounding

The ultimate technique is to increase your rate of return *and* let your money compound. The following chart reflects an investment of *$100 per month* at 5 percent, 8 percent, and 12 percent for four different periods.

Years	5%	8%	12%
10	$15,528	$18,295	$23,004
20	$41,103	$58,902	$98,926
30	$83,225	$149,035	$349,496
40	$152,602	$349,101	$1,176,477

The following chart shows the results of a **lump-sum investment of $10,000** at 5 percent, 8 percent, and 12 percent.

Years	5%	8%	12%
10	$16,289	$21,589	$31,058
20	$26,533	$46,610	$96,463
30	$43,219	$100,627	$299,599
40	$70,400	$217,245	$930,510

These charts reveal the importance of making your money work harder for you. Whether you are saving monthly for retirement or have a lump sum to invest, you *must* make the proper choices to stay ahead of the game.

Chapter 5

Investment classes: Your key to financial success

Where you ultimately end up financially is based on three factors: how much you choose to put away for retirement; whether or not you choose to withdraw any of that money along the way; and how you choose to invest that retirement money. This chapter addresses the third factor: investing your money.

There are a wide array of investment vehicles. But as a rule, you will invest your retirement money in the three most common: cash and cash equivalents, stocks, and bonds. If you understand how each of these fits into your retirement plans, you will know just about everything you need to achieve retirement security.

The more you earn

It might be hard to believe, but in many cases, the amount of money you will have at retirement is more dependent upon the rate of return you receive than the amount of money you invest. Now, that might be an over-simplification, but let's look at an example.

John and Mary work for the same company. They are both 40 years old and plan to retire at 60. John is putting

$100 a month in his 401(k) plan and is investing that money in the growth accounts. Mary is putting $200 a month away but investing hers in the guaranteed account. Assume John earns the long-term average of 10 percent and Mary earns 5 percent. How much money will each have in 20 years?

John will have $75,936. Mary will have $82,206. You can see that Mary will have $6,270 more than John, but she has invested $24,000 more. Turning it around, John will have contributed $24,000 less than Mary but will only have $6,270 less!

Take a look at the following chart. It shows the results of a $10,000 investment in various asset classes (taking into account inflation) over the past 20 years. Look at the difference a higher rate of return makes:

$10,000 Investment 12/31/77	Value 12/31/97	Annual Rate
3-month CDs	$43,607	7.64%
Long Term Govt. Bonds	$72,682	10.43%
S&P 500 Index	$217,570	16.65%
Dow Jones Industrials	$211,141	16.47%
Consumer Price Index	$26,070	4.91%

(Note: I have included the Consumer Price Index, which is the inflation rate. You can see that the cost of living has gone up an average of 4.91 percent per year for the past 20 years. I have included this figure to let you see how various investments have performed relative to the cost of living. One goal of investing is to receive a rate of return, after taxes, greater than the inflation rate.)

Which would you rather have, $43,607 or $217,570? Let me give you a hint: When given the choice between two piles of money, take the most valuable pile! Now, I know that there is such a thing as risk, which you must consider. But you must also be careful about cheating yourself out of a better return by making the wrong choices. To help you put it together, let me explain the various asset classes and show you that understanding how they work will be a big factor toward achieving your retirement dreams.

Cash equivalents

Most of the money in this country is in banks, savings banks, and credit unions. These financial institutions provide a high degree of safety, reliability, and convenience. They are fines place for your emergency money, as well as *some* of your longer-term savings. However, these institutions are not the place to accumulate wealth.

Cash equivalents include savings accounts, certificates of deposit, money market accounts, and the guaranteed (fixed) accounts in retirement plans. Most people tend to gravitate toward this category because it is considered "safe." This means that the principal will always be there. You might not get much in the way of rate of return, but at least you won't lose any money, and that's a comforting thought. But there's a cost.

Financially successful people don't let their money rest in a bank very long. If they do, it is in small amounts. Financially challenged people, on the other hand, leave everything there forever because they are afraid of taking any risks. In addition, they want it "available" in case they need money. If this is your comfort level, then you have fallen into the "insured equals safety" trap the banks have set for you.

The safety trap

Actually, several factors contribute to this trap being so effective. The first is that we all tend to be loss-adverse. In other words, all things being equal, we'd rather not lose our money. I'm going to tell you how that misconception is hurting you. The second reason is most people don't know enough about investing in other asset classes to feel comfortable. I'll also take care of that if you stick with me.

Let's start out with a basic fact: You won't get rich keeping your money in the bank. Of course, you won't lose your money, either. But you will lose buying power, because it will be reduced by taxes and inflation.

Losing your money

What's wrong with keeping your money in the bank? Nothing, as long as you don't go overboard. Everyone needs to have *some* money in the bank. The problem is that if you have *too much* there, you are losing money unnecessarily to taxes, inflation, and low interest rates.

Let me give you an example. You put $10,000 into a 5 percent certificate of deposit. As a result, you receive $500 in interest. However, that amount is taxable. Assume a 30 percent loss of interest to taxes. That's $150 gone forever. You net $350 after you pay your taxes. However, the cost of living continues to go up. It has averaged 4.91 percent per year for the past 20 years. That means that you must reduce the interest you receive by that percentage, or $491 per year. So in reality, after taxes and inflation, you actually *lost* $141 that year by keeping your money in the bank. Doesn't sound so good to me.

A very important concept to grasp is the advantage of earning a higher rate of return on your money. Notice that I didn't say earning higher "interest." There is a big difference between the two.

Look at return, not interest

Too many people think in terms of how much "interest" they are earning. Your mind-set is all wrong if, when looking at a mutual fund, you ask your financial advisor, "How much interest will I make?" You are thinking the way bankers want you to think. You assume that your money is going to grow in a straight line, the only variable being how fast.

However, that's not the way to create financial independence. As I continue with this very important chapter, I will talk about other assets classes: places where you have the opportunity to substantially increase your wealth.

Bonds

Bonds are issued by governments (state, local, federal), and corporations who want to borrow money. They promise to you your money back at a certain date. In the meantime, they will pay you interest.

Some bonds even have tax advantages. U.S. Government bonds are not subject to state and local income taxes. State and local bonds (called tax-free) are not subject to federal income taxes, and if they are issued by your state, not subject to your state income taxes.

Sound good? Well, sort of. But over time, bonds don't perform as well as some other asset classes we're going to discuss. And bonds with long maturities (10 years and longer) can be very volatile in price.

Can't lose?

The problem is that people think they can't lose money in bonds. Well, that's a fallacy. You can lose money. First of all, the issuer might default. That is rare, but it does happen. The bigger risk is that interest rates will rise, and when you want to sell your bond, you might get less than you paid.

For example, let's assume that in September 1998 you buy a Treasury bond paying 5 percent interest. That means that each year for 30 years you will receive $2,500 in interest ($1,250 paid two times a year). But what happens in 10 years when you have an emergency and need your money back? Will you get your $50,000 back? Maybe, maybe not.

Rising rates

Let's assume that in 10 years, interest rates are 8 percent. That means new $50,000 bonds are paying $4,000 a year, compared to the $2,500 yours is getting. You go to sell your $50,000 bond. Will you get your $50,000 back? No way! Why would anyone pay $50,000 and accept $2,500 per year interest when they can take the same money and get $4,000? So you'll have to take less than $50,000.

That's the trouble with long-term bonds. When interest rates go up, the market value of your bond goes down. Of course, the opposite is also true: When rates go down, bond prices go up.

But bonds do provide diversification. The older you are, the more of your money you will want in bonds. But I recommend short-term bonds—bonds maturing in an average of two to five years. That gives you most of the interest rate of a long-term bond without the volatility.

I use bonds to provide stability to portfolios of my retired clients. As we will see when we get into actual asset allocation, you will want to be well-diversified, and the older you are, the more conservative you will want to be.

Common stock

You will get the greatest long-term returns by investing in the best companies in the world. You do this by purchasing common stock. You can buy individual stocks or invest in mutual funds. I will discuss mutual funds in the next chapter.

When you buy stock, you are buying ownership in a company. So if you purchase shares in Intel, you own part of the company—a small part—but at least a part! For example, as of this writing, Intel has 353,532,400 shares of stock outstanding. If you purchase one share, you own 1/353,532,400th of Intel. It's not much, but everyone has to start somewhere.

Why invest?

Why do people invest in stock? Two reasons: dividends and capital gains. Dividends are paid by a company when they feel they can give some of their money back to the shareholders. Capital gains are achieved, for example, when you purchase shares of Intel for $10,000 and sell them later for $15,000. That $5,000 profit is called a capital gain.

Under our tax scheme, capital gains are divided into two classes. The taxes on long-term capital gains, which include any asset held for at least 12 months, are capped at 20 percent (10 percent for people in the 15-percent tax bracket), whereas short-term capital gains, which re assets held for less than 12 months, are capped at 28 percent. Both of these compare very favorably to a top income tax rate of 39.5 percent for ordinary income and dividends.

Whereas dividends once played an important part for a lot of people, they have dwindled in importance for several reasons. First, people realize that the big benefit in stocks is the gain in the value, not any dividend you may receive.

But second, look at what I just told you about the top tax rates on dividends and capital gains. You can see that receiving income in the form of capital gains is much more favorable than receiving it in the form of dividends.

Not a casino

What keeps people from investing in the stock market is that they see it as a giant casino, where you roll the dice and take your chances. Nothing could be further from the truth. The stock market is just a mechanism for the convenience of companies who want to sell shares in their company to the public, and the public who wants to invest in the best companies in the world. Some markets, such as the New York Stock Exchange (NYSE), are a centralized location where this trading takes place. And for companies not traded on the exchange, there is a computerized system. It is referred to as the "over-the-counter market." You may recognize it as NASDAQ. It is an automated system where trades take place instantaneously. It's a "virtual" stock exchange. In either case, whether you buy General Electric on the NYSE, or Intel on NASDAQ, you have a very liquid investment that is easy to buy and sell.

Statistical look

The best way to view the stock market is over a long period of time. Although you must remember that past performance doesn't guarantee future results, you can draw some conclusions from studying long periods of time.

Since 1926, the stock market has averaged 11 percent per year. Since 1940, the market has gone up in 41 years and gone down in 17 years. That's up 70 percent of the time. Does that sound like a crap shoot to you?

Now I run into people all the time who say that they don't invest in the stock market because either 1) they have lost money in the market, 2) a friend has lost money in the market, or 3) because the market is "too high."

Well, saying you're not going to invest in the market because you've lost money is like saying you're not going to drive a car because you've had an accident. But that's not the point. How, when the market has averaged 11 percent a year and gone up 70 percent of the time over most of our lifetimes, can you lose money in the market? As I see it, only for one of two, reasons:

1. You've bought bad stocks and sold them at a loss.
2. You've panicked out of the market before it went back up.

That's about it. Let's look at each one. If number one is true, if you've lost money buying individual stocks, then don't buy individual stocks. I feel that the best course for the average person is to invest in a well-diversified, well-managed mutual fund. That will take care of problem number one.

Reason number two is very common. People hate to invest when the market is so high. Well, let's face reality: The market has been up in 70 percent of the years since 1940. That means that 70 percent of the time, the market is "too high" for those people. And the other 30 percent of the time, when the market is down, the same people are scared out of investing by the news media. So they never invest. And in so doing, they miss out on untold possible wealth.

If you have a long-range outlook, then it doesn't matter where the market is today, it only matters where it is going to be in five to 10 years. And because it will probably be up, then it is always a good time to invest.

"What if the market goes down and never goes back up?" If this sounds like something you'd say, you're concerned about something that has never happened before. You are concerned that if you invest, you're going to lose all your money. In other words, the next market decline is going to be permanent. The market will never go back up. (I heard that a lot in 1998.)

Temporary declines

Statistics show that all market declines are temporary. Now, temporary can mean different things to different people. I use "temporary" as the opposite of "permanent." A permanent decline means that the market goes down and never goes back up. A temporary decline means that it eventually goes back up.

Since 1940, the past 58 years, the market has gone up 70 percent of the time. That means, by definition, that every single decline we've had since then has been temporary. And, in fact, that's true back to the beginning of our stock market. Every decline has proven to be temporary.

Don't get me wrong, even a temporary decline can be painful, especially if it lasts for most of a decade, as happened in the 1970s. However, people who stuck through the terrible 70s made tons of money in the 80s and 90s.

Therefore, the only way you lose money, over time, is to think a temporary decline is really a permanent decline. But because that has never happened in this country before, then it really isn't something to worry about.

Lose all your money?

Most of us spend too much time worrying about things that will never happen. Losing all your money in the stock market is one of them. People ask me all the time, "Can I lose all my money in this fund?" The answer is yes, if every stock in the fund goes to zero. So let's assume you're invested in the Standard & Poor's 500 fund. This fund comprises the 500 largest companies in America. Can you lose all of your money? Here's what has to happen. All the stocks in the portfolio have to go to zero. The top 10 companies alone are: General Electric, Microsoft, Exxon, Coca-Cola, Intel, Merck, Royal Dutch Petroleum, IBM, Philip Morris, Procter & Gamble. That's just the 10 largest. There are 490 more behind them.

So let me ask you a question: Do you think that all of those companies will go to zero? Of course not. And if they did, if virtually every corporation in America is worthless, what do you think would happen to your FDIC-insured bank accounts? You can bet that the insurance won't cover the losses. So let's face reality. Don't worry about something that has virtually no probability of happening. Instead, focus on what has a greater chance of happening, and that is the greatest companies in the world will continue to grow and prosper, creating the wealth you are seeking.

Not for everyone

That said, the stock market is not for everyone. Obviously, although over the long term the market has done well, you might not want to have to wait that long. You might have a shorter time frame. And if in fact that is true, then the stock market is not the place for you.

But before you pass off the market as not the place for you because you are close to retirement—or beyond—remember one fact I mentioned in the first chapter. If you are 55 and married, statistics show one of you will make it to age 90. That's 35 more years. If you're 65, chances are you'll live another 20 years or so. That's not short term, that's long term. Prices can go up an awful lot in just 20 years.

Let's go back 20 years and suppose that you retired in 1978 on a fixed income of $20,000 per year. That was plenty of money back then. Today, to buy what $20,000 per year would have bought you back then, you would need $52,000 per year! That's why you need to think long term even if you're retired. The difference is, however, that as you get older, you tend to be more conservative in your investments. But nevertheless, the need for growth still exists. And that's why you need to still be invested in the best companies in the world.

The best way for most people to invest in the stock market is though managed money, preferably mutual funds.

Chapter 6

Mutual funds: Diversification is the answer

This chapter deals with mutual funds, my preferred method of investing retirement funds. The important thing about this chapter is that it also applies to the fund choices in your retirement plan.

You've heard a lot about mutual funds over the past years. In fact, you've probably invested in them, if not individually, then through your retirement plan at work. That's right, the choices in your 401(k) plan and tax-sheltered annuity are, in fact, mutual funds.

A mutual fund is an investment company that accepts money from individuals, then pools that money and invests it. The fund may be invested in stocks, bonds, or some combination, depending upon its stated objective. Mutual funds are for people who, for one reason or another, don't want to take the risk or time of selecting stocks and bonds themselves. In other words, they would rather let professionals manage their money for them.

Why invest in mutual funds?

There are three primary reasons why people invest in mutual funds instead of buying individual stocks:

1. **Diversification.** If you own shares of one company, and that company's stock takes a big drop, you will suffer a major loss. However, if you own shares of a mutual fund that invests in hundreds of companies, then a similar drop in a particular stock should be insignificant.

2. **Professional management.** We stated earlier how difficult it is to pick good companies on a continuing basis. Fund managers can't always do this either, but at least they have the resources to get information.

3. **Affordability.** Unlike investments in individual stocks and bonds, mutual funds allow you to start with purchases as low as $25. You may also make automatic drafts or additional contributions in amounts as low as $25.

Types of mutual funds

There are as many kinds of mutual funds as there are classifications of investments. The primary ones we need to know about are bond funds and stock funds.

Bond Funds invest in three types of bonds: government, corporate, and tax-free. Some funds invest specifically in one type of these instruments, others mix them. It all depends on the objective of the fund. You need to know that like bonds themselves, bond funds will fluctuate based on interest rates. As rates go up, bond prices go down, and vice versa. That's why I prefer short term (two to five years) for bond funds. They capture most of the yield with a minimum amount of risk. Bonds are for people who are risk adverse. The older and more conservative you are, the more money you will have in bonds.

Stock funds, unlike bond funds, are very diverse. This is what causes so much confusion. There are thousands of different funds out there with a lot of different objectives. This confusion leads people to make the wrong choices when it comes to choosing and investing in their retirement accounts.

There are many types of stock funds. *Balanced* funds invest in a combination of stocks and bonds, providing growth with reduced risk. *Income* funds invest in companies that pay high dividends (probably including some bonds). *Equity-income* funds invest in companies that are expected to provide growth in addition to paying dividends, such as established companies. *Index* funds invest in the same stocks, and in the same percentage, as the various indices, such as the Standard & Poor's 500. *Growth* funds invest in companies with a good record of growth and potential for above-average returns. *Aggressive growth* funds invest in smaller companies that are expected to experience above-average growth. *Global* funds invest in both the United States and internationally. *International* funds invest in companies outside the United States. *Natural resource* and *precious metals* funds invest in companies engaged in the various aspects of natural resources (oil, gas, industrial metals) and precious metals (primarily gold and silver).

How you make money

Mutual funds are only as good as the investments they make. They fluctuate in value with the stocks and bonds they own. If everything goes well, you make money from three sources: dividends, capital gains, and increasing share values.

Dividends

Companies in which the mutual funds invest pay interest (if they are bonds) and possibly dividends (if they are stocks) to the mutual fund. The degree of emphasis on dividends depends on whether the fund is a bond fund or a stock fund, and whether it is designed for income or for growth. The mutual fund turns around and pays them to you. You have a choice in how you wish to receive them. You may reinvest them in additional shares of the fund, or you may have the fund pay the dividends to you in cash.

Capital gains

When the mutual fund sells stocks or bonds that are in its portfolio, there is either a gain or a loss. The fund balances the gains and losses and pays you a "capital gains distribution." The amount of capital gains depends on the type of fund. If you own mutual funds outside a tax-sheltered retirement plan, then you will be happy that the government recently reduced the taxes on capital gains to a maximum of 20 percent on long-term capital gains (10 percent if you are in the 15 percent federal tax bracket). Once again, you can receive capital gains distributions in cash or reinvest them in additional shares of the fund.

Increase in value

People who aren't seeking income invest in mutual funds to achieve growth. Stocks have historically appreciated nicely, with obvious fluctuations along the way. Stock mutual funds are a way of participating in this growth.

You will obviously achieve greater growth if you allow your dividends and capital gains to accumulate rather than taking them out. Remember what I talked about in Chapter 4: Leaving your dividends and capital gains in the fund takes advantage of compound interest. It's important to understand that the name of the game when it comes to mutual fund investing is to accumulate as many *shares* as you can. You do this by reinvesting, not spending, your dividend and capital gains distributions.

Buying mutual funds

Purchasing mutual funds is probably the easiest, least complicated way to invest. There are two ways to do this: You can purchase them from the mutual fund company or you can go through a broker or investment advisor.

1. **Direct purchase.** You can invest in mutual funds directly through the fund itself. These funds are called *no-loads* because they don't charge a sales commission (although some direct firms, such as Fidelity, do charge front-end fees on some of their mutual funds). You find the fund you want, call a toll-free number, and ask them to send you information. You then complete the paperwork, send it back with your money, and voilà, you're the proud owner of the fund. Because it's illegal for the phone representatives to provide investment advice unless they are licensed (relatively few are), you are on your own for the major decisions. However, much of the information in this book will help you.

2. **Investment firms.** You might not want to have to do the research and pick the funds yourself. You might want someone to make these decisions for you. In this case, you go to a stockbroker or an independent investment advisor. They are compensated by the mutual fund company, however *you* really pay for their advice, as I'll show you shortly.

53

Mutual fund fees

There are primarily four types of mutual funds: front-end loads, back-end loads, level-loads, and no-loads. Let's look at each.

1. **Front-end load** funds, usually called "A" shares, include a fee with each purchase. This is typically anywhere between 3 and 6 percent, with a few charging as much as 8 percent. There is no fee when you redeem your shares.

2. **Back-end load** funds, often sold as "B" shares, don't carry an up-front commission, but they do have a "contingent deferred sales charge." This means that if you sell shares within the first five to seven years, there is a decreasing sales charge on the redeemed principal. For example, the deferred sales charge might be 5 percent on shares redeemed during the first year, 4 percent the second, 3 percent the third, and so on until it disappears. These fees generally don't apply to your earnings. However, you do pay higher ongoing fees than in the "A" shares.

3. **Level-load** funds, often sold as "C" shares, charge nothing up-front and no redemption fee, as long as you hold your shares at least 12 months. However, you do pay higher ongoing fees than in "A" or "B" shares.

4. **No-load** funds carry no front-end or back-end fees. When sold through investment professionals, that person or firm usually charges an annual fee.

12b-1 fees

Many funds include a special fee that they can use for any number of purposes. This is called a 12b-1 fee. The funds that distribute their shares through investment professionals use these fees to help reimburse that person for his services. The funds that sell their shares through discount brokerage firms can use these fees to reimburse that brokerage firm for the services that they say they are offering "free" to their clients.

The fee usually starts at .25 percent and can go up to 1 percent, especially in the case of "B" and "C" shares. So on a $100,000 portfolio, this fee will range anywhere from $250 per year to $1,000 per year.

Many people think that no-loads don't charge 12b-1 fees, but that's not necessarily true. Many do charge them because it is a way for them to reimburse themselves for advertising fees or to reimburse the discount brokers for handling their shares.

Which fee method is best?

The best method for you depends on whether you want to make all the decisions yourself or you wish to leave those decisions up to a professional. I find that most financially successful people are willing to pay for advice if that advice increases the chances of their success.

There is a continual disagreement between advocates of what I call "help" (load) and "no-help" (no load) funds. While nobody wants to pay a fee, that should not be your main consideration. Rather, you should concentrate on whether you want to work with a financial professional and pay some type of fee, or make the decisions yourself and pay no fee. That should be based solely on how comfortable you are with your own ability to make investment decisions. If you feel that you need help, recognize that brokers and planners can provide valuable assistance. If the advice you get is worthwhile, then it is worth the cost. If that advice helps you achieve your financial goals, then the effect of the fee over time will prove to be negligible. If, on the other hand, you feel comfortable handling your own investments, by all means do it yourself and save the fee. The key is whether or not you need advice and assistance.

No-loads through advisors

A relatively new phenomenon is investment advisors offering no-load funds. That is the way most of my retired clients invest. For a fee I provide my clients with ongoing financial advice and service along with excellent products. So now they have the best of both worlds. You can enjoy those same benefits. I'll tell you how to find a good financial advisor in the following chapter.

Chapter 7

Advice givers: The good, the bad, and the ugly

Advice. We all love to give it. Sometimes we love to receive it. The problem is that most of the advice we receive, especially financial, is worthless and counterproductive.

I break advisors down into three categories: the good, the bad, and the ugly. Let me describe each before I delve into them in more detail.

The Good are the people who give you advice that is in your best interests. This group is made up of those "professionals" (brokers, financial planners, and investment advisors) who put your interests first, above their own. It consists of "amateurs" (friends, acquaintances, relatives) who are successful in their own right, and who share that success with you in the form of excellent advice.

The Bad are those people who are just in it for the money. They don't care one bit about you; they just want to sell you something so they can pay their own bills.

The Ugly is the largest group. These people are the "professionals" who give what turns out to be bad advice, but don't do it maliciously—they just aren't competent. It also includes those "amateurs" who really don't know what they are talking about but like to tell you what to do anyway. Financial publications can fall into this category because some of their advice lacks consistency from issue to issue. Let me explain each in more detail, working backward.

The ugly

A lot of your friends and co-workers are filled with good intentions, but many of them are what I call "financial losers." Now, I'm not using this as a derogatory term but more of a descriptive one. These folks live from one day to the next, accumulating little in the way of investments or retirement funds. They are up to their eyeballs in debt, yet think they know exactly what *you* need to do to be financially successful. You know people like this. You may even have a few as relatives or co-workers. Here's one of my simpler rules: Don't take advice from financial losers.

Her father said...

Some time ago, a couple came into my office for a consultation. They were in their 50s and were finally starting to think about retirement. In the course of our discussion, I brought up the subject of equities, explaining that they might consider investing part of their assets in a good-quality fund with professional management that could provide a better return than the bank.

At that point the wife said, "My father told me never to invest in the stock market. He told me to keep all my money in the bank." My response was simply, "What kind of financial condition is your father in?" She responded that he had passed away a few years before. When I asked what kind of financial condition he was in when he died, she said, "He died broke."

Now, I certainly wasn't going to say anything about her father, because it was his right to choose how to invest his own money. I'm not even saying that he was wrong in his advice, because his advice was based on his viewpoint. My point is this: She took advice from a man who died penniless. Did that really make sense for her?

My advisor said...

My wife, Nancy, and I recently purchased a condo on the ocean. Now, I don't know a thing about real estate, so I would never choose a real estate investment on what *I* thought was best. But I will listen to the "right" person. A good friend of mine—a successful, knowledgeable real estate investor—recommended that we purchase this unit. Over the years he had made a lot of money on his real estate investments and was purchasing two units himself. On his recommendation we went ahead, and it has proven to be a wise investment.

A lot of people think they know what is right, it's just that they have never done it themselves. I would never take advice from these folks. But when a successful person tells me what I should do, and he's doing it himself, I am more than willing to listen.

Well-meaning brokers

Friends, relatives, and co-workers aren't your only problem. There are also a number of well-meaning financial advisors and brokers who just give bad advice. They don't do this on purpose. They may even have good intentions, but they just don't do a really good job for their clients. They jump from one investment to another. They continually call you up telling you to sell something and buy something else. They always come to you with the hot product of the day from their firm. These people, like well-meaning friends, should be avoided.

One word of caution. The recent stock market boom has brought a lot of new stockbrokers into the business. These are primarily good people, but they don't have much experience. Until 1998, they never experienced a major market drop. They only saw the market go straight up. I would be careful about people who are young, inexperienced, and overly enthusiastic about the market.

Financial publications

I have some concern when it comes to financial magazines, especially with their mutual fund recommendations. The biggest problem is that they tend to recommend different mutual funds each issue. So how are you to know what to do when "The Top 10 Funds for Retirement" this month are different from "The Best Funds for You" six months ago?

You can't assume all the recommended funds are best for your particular situation. As we will see when we talk about risk tolerance, every fund has a different level of risk. And each person has a different risk tolerance. How can you know that those 10 funds are all best for you? And, if not, how do you pick which ones are?

Mutual fund advertisements

Another problem deals with mutual fund advertisements. Leaf through any publication and you will see ads from mutual funds trumpeting their performance. You look at the numbers and they really look great. The problem is, once again, those numbers don't address the issue of risk. It's great that a fund has averaged 18 percent for 10 years, but what if you can't assume that much risk? Beyond that, past performance is no guarantee of future results. Be careful, and don't get sucked into the performance game.

Part-timers

The other people I would be concerned about are the part-time financial salespeople. These are the teachers, coaches, corporate employees, etc., who sell insurance and investments in their spare time. I know I would never take financial advice from a person who lacks training and experience, and I certainly wouldn't listen to someone who is doing it part time. After all, if they are that good, why are they only doing it part-time? If I'm going to pay someone to help me, I want the best!

The bad

Unfortunately, the world is full of crooks. Being a financial advisor and radio personality, I pay particular attention to the people literally trying to steal your money. I hear their ads on the radio, I see them on television. I get their junk in the mail. These are the folks who call you on the phone from who-knows-where with a "can't miss" investment. They especially take advantage of older people. They run advertisements telling you about all the money you're going to make in heating oil and gold.

Let's face facts. The person who calls doesn't care one bit about you. Let me explain a very important fact about the investment business. I am required, by law, to know my clients' financial condition. That means that before I can recommend an investment, I need to make sure that it is suitable for the person, just like a doctor must diagnose your illness before prescribing medication.

Now, let's compare that to the person who interrupts your dinner with a "great deal." He doesn't know a thing about you. He doesn't know your income, your assets, your risk tolerance, and most important—your goals. He only knows one thing: He must make a sale to someone, and it might as well be you. In other words, he isn't doing what's best for you, he's doing what's best for him.

The rules

The rules here are very simple:

1. Don't ever, ever, ever, ever buy anything over the phone from somebody you don't know.

2. If you get an unsolicited phone call from a brokerage firm, or any direct marketing company, tell them to take you off their list and hang up.

3. Don't ever respond to a radio or television ad pushing options, commodities, futures, or any other get-rich-quick scheme. I promise you one thing: You will lose your money. If you don't lose it with your first investment, you will eventually lose it. Statistics prove me right on that.

4. Don't let a broker "churn" your account. In other words, don't let him create a lot of buying and selling in your account. He will be the only one who makes money on that deal.

The good

This category consists of financially successful friends and acquaintances and honorable brokers and financial advisors. If you are going to take advice from anyone, this is the group you want to listen to.

If you have friends or relatives who are financially successful, then by all means listen to them. But be careful about the term "financially successful." I'm not talking about the person who drives a luxury car, has a huge home with a big mortgage, takes lavish vacations, and wears expensive jewelry. I'm talking about the person who is financially secure because he is smart with his money. A lot of people make a good living, but most of them spend all that money and more. The financially secure people are careful with their spending habits and wise with their investments.

The financial service industry has lots of fine people who can provide good advice. But you have to approach this with caution because the industry is full of people who also fit into the bad and ugly categories. So I'm going to tell you what to look for.

Compensation

People in the financial services industry get paid one of three ways: by commission, by fee, or a combination of the two. One way or the other, they are going to get paid. There's nothing wrong with that. They, like you, don't work for free.

As I discussed in the previous chapter, you first have to decide if you want to work with someone or go it alone. Let's assume that you've decided to pay for financial advice. After all, financially successful people are willing to pay for advice if it increases their chances of success, so why shouldn't you?

So, again, these guys gotta get paid. If they derive their income via a commission, that means that they are going to get paid up-front every time they sell you something. If you buy a stock, or a mutual fund, or an annuity, or a bond, they are going to get a commission. There's nothing wrong with this. If you go to a doctor for an operation, he, too, is going to be paid a commission. Of course, he doesn't call it that, but it's the same thing.

Impartiality?

There is, of course, a problem with dealing with a commission financial advisor. That involves lack of impartiality. How can he give you impartial advice if he is going to make money from what he tells you to do? Of course, that could be said of your dentist or your doctor. Your dentist is going to make money by telling you that you need a filling, or your teeth cleaned, or your teeth capped. So it could be said your dentist isn't impartial, either.

And, of course, this is correct. A person who makes a commission by getting you to invest in what he is showing you isn't going to be impartial. That's why I'm not thrilled by this kind of compensation.

You have to understand the nature of the financial industry. Brokers, just like you, have to make a living. They do this by selling products. Once they sell you something, they move on to someone else, and to someone else after that. It is a never-ending cycle. And therein lies the problem: How can they provide you with good service? How can they give your account full attention if they are busy trying to generate new business? Of course, they can't. That's the problem.

The other method of compensation is via a fee. Personally, I favor this approach. Fee advisors get paid one of two ways: a flat fee for services performed, or a fee based on the assets under management. Different advisors have their preferences. I do it both ways, but most of my clients' fees are based on the value of their accounts. That way, I make more if my clients make more; I make less if my clients don't do as well.

This is how you want to be treated

The first thing you want to do is interview several financial advisors. Here is a short checklist of what you want from anyone you interview. You should be able to answer yes to these questions.

- Did he treat you with respect?
- Did he ask about your concerns and goals and pay close attention to the answers?
- Did he explain things simply and to your satisfaction?
- Did he talk to you as an equal, as opposed to talking down to you and making you feel stupid?
- Was he relaxed in his approach?
- Were you encouraged to think about it and not pushed into any decision?
- Did he talk about your needs and not his products?

I think you can probably tell if someone is trying to push you into something as opposed to looking at your best interests. Just don't let anyone push you into something you don't feel comfortable with. You have the ultimate weapon—you can say *no*!

What you want your financial advisor to be

I recently surveyed a number of my top clients. The survey included a question about what they thought about me as their advisor. I want to share what they said with you, not to brag, but because these are the kinds of things you want from your financial advisor. I have left them in their words:

- "I have the sense that if you call me, you have my best interests in mind."

- "You are knowledgeable—very well educated."

- "You're very patient; you don't make me feel dumb. And you explain everything very well."

- "Your sense of humor; you're good with people."

- "You stay in touch with us."

- "You seem to be concerned with our welfare."

- "You give advice, but you don't stomp them to take that advice."

- "You make things understandable."

- "You're really interested in your clients' interests, not just business..."

- "We can expect a straightforward honest answer that we're looking for."

Again, I provide you this information in the hopes that it will give you an idea of what you deserve from your financial advisor. You are paying for advice; you are paying for service. Don't let anyone get away with giving you less than you deserve.

The services they provide

Finally, I want to share with you the types of services you should receive from your investment advisor. So you'll know what's available, here are just some of the services I provide to my fee clients:

- Unbiased advice because I'm compensated by a fee.

- Comprehensive financial management services.

- Predetermined annual fee.

- Portfolio customized to their needs, time horizon, and risk tolerance.
- Full-time financial advisor—clients can call anytime.
- Quarterly meetings for performance review and education.
- Tax planning.
- Personal relationship.
- Performance reporting/goal monitoring.
- Goal-setting and follow-through.

You deserve the best

The financial world is filled with some really good planners. There's no reason you shouldn't avail yourself of one of these people. Now that you know what you should be looking for, go out and find someone who can provide you with the service you need, and you deserve. And don't let anyone talk you into anything less.

Chapter 8

Social Security: Will it or won't it?

I tell my younger clients not to depend on Social Security for their retirement. My feeling is that if you are at least in your 50s, Social Security will be there for you. More of it might be subject to income taxes, there may be income tests to determine if you should get it at all, but it should be there for those who need it. If you are younger, then you'd better not depend on it.

Let me answer the most common questions I get from my clients and from seminar attendees about Social Security as it applies to retirement benefits.

Who is covered?

Most working people are covered by Social Security. It is easier to identify those who are not covered: federal employees hired before January 1984; railroad employees covered under the Railroad Retirement System; state employees covered under their own retirement program; clergy who opt not to participate; employees of many school systems operating under older rules; and those who have not earned enough to qualify. If your payroll stub does not have an entry for "FICA Withholding," then you are not covered under Social Security.

How do I qualify?

You qualify for Social Security benefits by acquiring sufficient "quarters of coverage" to be considered *fully insured* or *currently insured.* In general, you receive "quarters of coverage" by having the required wages, or self-employment income, in any calendar quarter.

The number of credits you need to get retirement benefits depends upon your date of birth. If you were born in 1929 or later, you need 40 credits (that's 10 years of work). If you were born before 1929, you need fewer than 40 credits. You subtract one credit for every year you were born before 1929.

How much will I get at retirement?

This is, of course, the number-one question. It's a difficult one to answer with any degree of accuracy. When I run retirement projections, the computer program I use gives me the option of using estimated benefits, or no benefits. However, I recommend that my clients get the official estimate directly from the Social Security Administration. All you have to do is call 800-772-1213 and ask for a *Request for Earnings Benefit Statement.* This form will allow Social Security to provide you with a full earnings history plus an estimate of your benefits based on different retirement ages.

When can I start receiving Social Security?

You are entitled to retirement benefits if you are fully insured and have reached the age of 62, or if you are a widow or widower and are age 60. If you begin receiving

Social Security at 62, you will receive a reduced benefit. For full benefits, you must refrain from taking benefits until the normal retirement age of 65. Be aware, however, that the "normal retirement age" will change in the years ahead.

What will be the normal retirement age?

To find out what yours will be, find your year of birth on the following table:

Your year of birth	Your full retirement age
1937	65
1938	65 years and 2 months
1939	65 years and 4 months
1940	65 years and 6 months
1941	65 years and 8 months
1942	65 years and 10 months
1943-1954	66 years
1956	66 years and 2 months
1957	66 years and 4 months
1958	66 years and 8 months
1959	66 years and 10 months
1960	67 years

Even if your normal retirement age is past 65, you may still take reduced benefits at age 62.

How do I decide when to retire?

In the past, age 65 was the age when most people hoped to retire. That is no longer true for most Americans. More and more people are retiring, or hoping to retire, at younger ages.

Under current rules, if you retire before you turn 65, your monthly benefits are reduced by 5/9 of 1 percent for each month you retire before the age of 65, up to a maximum of 20 percent. That works out to be approximately 6.7 percent per year.

If you plan to start receiving benefits after age 62, Social Security suggests that you contact them in advance to see which month is the best to start claiming benefits. In some cases, your decision as to when to begin receiving benefits could make a difference in what you receive.

How do I sign up for benefits?

To get started, you can visit your local Social Security office or call Social Security's nationwide toll-free number: 800-772-1213.

Can I continue to work and receive benefits?

Possibly. Your earnings from a job won't affect your Social Security benefits *once you've reached age 70*. However, prior to 70, your benefits will be reduced if your earnings exceed a certain amount. Figures for 1998 follow:

If you are *65 through 69*, you can earn $14,500 without penalty. After that, $1 will deducted for each $3 you earn over the limit.

If you are *under 65*, you can earn $9,120 without penalty. After that, $1 in benefits will be deducted for each $2 you earn above the limit.

The good news is that the exempt amounts will increase in the years ahead. For recipients between the ages of 65 and 69, the exempt amount increases to $15,500 in 1999, $17,000 in 2000, $25,000 in 2001, and $30,000 in 2002.

There is a special provision that applies to your earnings in the year you retire only. In effect, it doesn't penalize you for earnings from your job if you retire mid-year. Social Security treats each month separately. Call the Social Security Administration and ask for the leaflet *How Work Affects Your Benefits* (Publication No. 05-10069). They will explain to you how it works.

What about Medicare?

Medicare is a government program that provides health insurance for persons 65 and older. In addition, some younger individuals who are receiving benefits under Social Security may be eligible. Coverage is divided into two parts:

1. **Part A** provides inpatient hospital care, inpatient skilled nursing facility care, home health care, and hospice care, subject to regulations.

2. **Part B** is voluntary and pays for doctors bills and a number of services not covered under Part A.

How do I get started?

If you already receiving Social Security benefits when you hit the age of 65, your Medicare Part A starts automatically. If you're not receiving benefits at that age, you need to sign up for Medicare. In either case, you must sign up for Part B if you want that coverage, and believe me, you do!

Chapter 9

Retirement plans: Follow the yellow brick road

If you work for a company that has a retirement plan, you are fortunate. However, if you don't participate in that retirement plan, you are wasting a golden opportunity to provide for your future security.

In the past, most employers totally funded their employees' retirement plans. However, all that has changed. The burden to provide for your retirement has been shifted to you.

If you want to retire with a lots of money, the best way to do it is through your employer's voluntary retirement plan. The primary benefits are *before-tax contributions* and *tax-deferred growth.*

Corporate retirement plans

There are a number of different plans available to corporate and government employees. Generally, your plan at work will fall within one of the following categories: pension, profit sharing, pretax savings—401(k), tax-sheltered annuity (403b), and deferred compensation (457). The contributions for pension and profit-sharing plans are made by your employer; the contributions for the other plans are made by you, possibly with some matching funds from your employer.

Tax-deductible contributions

If you are going to invest money, you want to do it with before-tax dollars. If you want to accumulate money the fastest way, you want to do it with tax-deferred dollars. Corporate retirement plans allow you to do both.

A before-tax contribution is money that you invest *before* it has been taxed. As a result, for a little more than $200, you can actually invest $300 in your retirement plan! How in the world do you do that? It's easy, just follow the math.

When you invest $300 pretax, you are investing the money *before* it is taxed. Let's assume you are in the 33 percent tax-bracket (28 percent federal plus some state or local taxes). Because the $300 you invested was before-tax, it was not included in your income. In other words, you don't have to pay current taxes on that $300 because you are going to put it away for your retirement.

So by not paying taxes, you actually save 33 percent of the $300, or $100, in taxes. By subtracting the $100 you saved in taxes from the $300 you invested in your retirement plan, you come up with $200. So for a cost of $200, you made a $300 investment in your retirement plan.

This is quite a benefit, and I'm not even including any money your employer may deposit as matching funds. If your employer is doing that, then your benefit is even greater!

Tax-deferred growth

The second benefit is tax-deferred growth. This means that the money you invest for your future grows without taxes until you choose to withdraw it. At that point, you pay taxes only on the amount you withdraw.

Taxes can be a big problem when you invest your money. That's because they can eat up 30 percent of your return. In your retirement plan, those taxes are deferred. Again, you don't pay any taxes until you choose to withdraw the money.

Real growth

Most people underestimate the value of tax-deferred growth, but I want to convince you of its real benefit. Let's assume you have the choice of investing $300 per month in your retirement plan or the same amount in a mutual fund outside your plan.

To make the comparison fair, we must realize that the money in the mutual fund goes in *after-tax*, but the deposit into 401(k) goes in *before-tax*. So we start with $300. If you don't put it in your retirement plan, you'll have to pay taxes on that money, approximately $100. Therefore, you really end up with $200 to invest, versus $300 if you put it in your retirement plan.

In addition, you are going to have to pay taxes every year on the mutual fund outside your plan. The stock market has averaged 11 percent per year since 1926. But a portion of this 11 percent is subject to dividend and capital gains taxes each year. To compensate for that, I will reduce the rate of return from 11 percent to 9 percent for the money outside the plan. I will continue to use 11 percent for the money in the plan, because taxes are deferred until withdrawal. That's because 1) the money wasn't tax-deductible when you invested it, and 2) you paid part of the taxes along the way.

Remember, however, that all the money in your retirement plan is subject to taxes when withdrawn. By comparison, only the growth on the mutual fund less any previously declared dividends and capital gains are subject to tax upon withdrawal. Let's look at the results:

Years Invested	Mutual Fund Outside Plan	Retirement Plan	Retirement Plan Advantage
5	$15,084	$23,855	$8,771
10	$38,703	$65,099	$26,396
15	$75,681	$136,407	$60,726
20	$133,577	$259,691	$126,114
25	$224,224	$472,840	$248,616
30	$366,149	$841,356	$475,207
35	$588,357	$1,478,489	$890,132

The advantage in the tax-deductible/tax-deferred account is both obvious and significant. You are making a big mistake if you don't contribute as much as you can to your employer's retirement plan...*and leave it there!*

Employer matching

I want to address one topic that causes a lot of people to make a terrible error, and that is the issue of employer matching. I just showed you that it is to your advantage to participate in your employer's retirement plan. Tax-deductible contributions and tax-deferred accumulation combine to provide you with an incredible benefit. But whenever I'm doing preretirement seminars at companies or counseling people in private, the issue of employer matching invariably comes up.

Some people tell me that they only contribute an amount that equals the amount their employer matches. Other people tell me that because their employer doesn't match, they don't contribute.

This thinking is just plain stupid. Look, you are responsible for your own retirement. The only money you have when you retire is the growth of the money you choose to put away today. If you choose not to contribute because your employer's not matching, who are you hurting? If you choose to only contribute 3 percent because that's all your employer's matching, who are you hurting?

The answer to both questions is the same, and it is obvious. You and only you (and your family) will suffer if you chose to not put away enough for your retirement. Therefore, why should your employer's decision to match or not match, or to match 3 percent or 12 percent, have any effect on what you do to prepare for your own retirement?

Anything your employer chooses to match is purely a bonus. In most cases, it's not going to have a material outcome on the amount of money you are going to have at retirement. Your contributions are going to be the primary determinant of what you have at retirement. Don't hurt yourself by doing something stupid. *You* prepare for your retirement. *You* choose how much money you will invest for your retirement. *You* enjoy the spoils, or suffer the consequences, of your actions.

Penalty for early withdrawals

Retirement plans provide for great retirement planning opportunities, but the tax laws are tough on you if you choose to take early withdrawals. Although the plans differ in technicalities, you are generally subject to a 10 percent premature distribution penalty if you take money out prior to age 59½. So, if you choose to take money out early, you will pay federal taxes (generally 28 percent), plus your state income taxes, if any, plus an additional 10 percent. That can be quite a sting. However, there are several exceptions to this 10-percent penalty. You don't have to pay the 10-percent early withdraw penalty if:

- You leave the company and you are age 55.
- You die or become disabled.
- The money is rolled over to another retirement plan.
- You pay deductible medical expenses that exceed 7.5 percent of your adjusted gross income.
- You receive money paid as the result of a qualified domestic relations court order (divorce).

Loans

The way a lot of people get around this penalty is to "borrow" money from their retirement plan. Various types of plans allow this, subject to a number of tough rules. The maximum amount you may borrow is the lesser of 50 percent of your balance or $50,000.

Once borrowed, your loan must be repaid over a five-year period, unless you borrow to purchase a home, in which case you have 10 years to repay. You must establish a payment schedule and adhere to it, otherwise, your loan becomes taxable. If you use the loan to purchase a home, the interest you pay is deductible. If you leave your employer and have a loan outstanding, you need to pay it back, or else it becomes taxable.

Personally, I think it is a terrible idea to borrow money from your retirement plan. You'll see why in Chapter 11.

Hardship withdrawals

Some plans allow hardship exemptions, allowing you to withdraw money for the purchase of a home, certain tuition payments, threat of eviction, or medical expenses. Always remember, however, that if you choose to use that money today, you lose both the money and potential growth on it for your retirement years. If you do qualify for a hardship exemption, you must still pay income taxes, plus the 10-percent IRS penalty if you are under age 59½.

Retirement

Upon retirement, you can withdraw your money (and possibly qualify for special averaging), or move it to an IRA Rollover account. An IRA Rollover is normally more advantageous because it defers the taxes until you start taking income. Unless you need cash immediately, it usually makes sense to roll it over.

If you receive your distribution yourself (as opposed to rolling it over), your employer must withhold 20 percent of it for taxes, even if you eventually move it into an IRA. I don't want to make this any more confusing than it already is, but if you do get that money, you do have 60 days in which to put it into an IRA. But the fact that your employer withheld 20 percent could be a problem.

For example, assume you withdraw the $400,000 from your 401(k). Your employer must withhold 20 percent for taxes, or $80,000. Therefore, you received a check for $320,000. You have 60 days to roll it over to avoid any taxes on the $400,000. But how much must you rollover to avoid taxes? The entire $400,000. How much did you receive? Only $320,000. If you want to avoid taxes (and maybe penalties), you must come up with that other $80,000. That's why it is so important to do everything right and not make any mistakes when filling out your paperwork.

To avoid this problem, and the withholding, simply do a "trustee to trustee" transfer. In other words, have your plan trustee transfer it directly to a new trustee. Employers have special forms for this, as do investment companies and banks.

Don't think of this 20 percent as a penalty, because it's really not. And don't figure that's all the tax you'll have to pay, because that's not true either. A lot of people I talk to think it's okay to get the money themselves, because it's only a 20 percent tax. Wrong! The amount you get from your retirement plan is subject to income taxes plus a penalty (if you are under the age of 55). The 20 percent is just a "down payment" on your taxes, not the whole amount.

Roth IRA

In my opinion, the Roth IRA is one of the best savings vehicles available. You can invest $2,000 into a Roth IRA each year. However, you do lose the ability to contribute to a Roth IRA if you earn too much. For example, if you are single, you may contribute to a Roth if your adjusted gross income is less than $95,000, but you may not contribute if it is more than $110,000. In between, you can make a proportionate contribution. Those figures are $150,000 and $160,000 for couples filing jointly. Participation in a corporate retirement plan does not affect your ability to participate in a Roth IRA.

Unlike traditional IRAs, where you must start taking money out after the age of 70½, there is no such requirement here. The money grows tax free and is never taxed, as long as you leave it in for at least five years after your initial deposit and experience one of the following:

1. Reach age 59½.
2. Become disabled.
3. First-time home purchase ($10,000 lifetime limit).
4. Die.

In addition, you have the right to convert a traditional IRA into a Roth IRA as long as your adjusted gross income is less than $100,000. Tax is due upon the conversion, but there is no 10-percent penalty. Congress established 1998 as the only year in which you could convert your IRA and spread your taxes over a four-year period. After that, all taxes are due in the year converted.

True benefits

IRAs, although small in scope, offer tremendous benefits that add up over the years. The Roth IRA, especially, can allow you to accumulate a significant sum of money.

If you've never participated in an IRA, and you can qualify income-wise, then by all means do it. And don't forget what I've told you about growth. Use the tax-deferred growth in a wisely invested IRA to pay off for you down the road.

Chapter 10

Retirement choices: The buck stops here

Your retirement plan consists of a variety of investment choices. You can choose from growth accounts, income accounts, guaranteed accounts, and possibly even your company's stock.

I strongly recommend that during your accumulation years you invest most of your money in growth accounts. Remember what I said about long-term growth: The stock market and mutual funds historically have outperformed most other choices over longer (10 years or more) periods of time.

In addition, because you are investing monthly, if the value drops, that just means that you will buy more shares or units for the same amount of money. Actually, it is better for your fund to go down while you're contributing. That means you are buying at lower prices. You will be taking advantage of a concept known as "dollar cost averaging." This is where you are able to buy more shares or units of your mutual fund or retirement account when the price drops. Remember, the name of the game is accumulating as many shares or units as you can.

Higher returns

If you are like most people, you are too conservative when it comes to investing your retirement money. You are afraid of losing money, so you pick the guaranteed accounts. Over the long run, this is a costly mistake. Remember, a secure retirement requires that you put away sufficient money, achieve high rates of return, and not take the money out early. Therefore, you need to invest the bulk of your retirement money in growth accounts.

Don't panic about market fluctuations and sudden drops in the stock market. In fact, if you're investing monthly, you actually want the market to go down so you can invest at lower prices.

If you are under age 40, you should be 100 percent in growth accounts. If you feel the need to be more conservative as you get older, you can start moving some money slowly from the growth to the fixed accounts. I'll show you how to invest your money in Chapter 13.

Your action and reaction

It's easy for me to tell you about how well the market's done over time and how much better it is to earn higher rates of return. And I showed you in Chapter 6 just how well you could have done, and can still do, by investing in the best companies in the world. But I also realize that emotionally you are still scared about investing in the stock market.

You're scared of losing your money. You're scared that you won't have enough money when you retire. You're scared of making the wrong decisions. You're scared that you may need the money and don't want to tie it up in your retirement account. And these feelings don't make you comfortable. I realize that. As a famous leader has been heard to say, "I feel your pain."

Consequences

But think of the pain if you don't do it. You retire. You don't have enough money to live comfortably. You have to get a job at McDonalds or Wal-Mart to make ends meet. Your friends are taking trips; you are sitting around doing nothing. You can't visit your children or grandchildren. You get scared that if you get sick, you will lose everything. You worry about what will happen if you go into a nursing home. You can't buy nice presents for your grandchildren because you can't afford to. You and your spouse are always arguing about money. You're blaming each other for your financial problems. You can't play golf with your friends. Your car is about to fall apart.

Sound pretty bad? Unfortunately it is the retirement that most Americans experience. I don't want that to happen to you. That's why I'm putting such a big emphasis on the need to contribute to your retirement plan, and the need to invest wisely.

Your investment choices

I know you want the best retirement possible, otherwise you wouldn't have read this far. So let's get familiar with the various investment choices found in most retirement plans.

Fixed account

This consists of money markets, short-term bonds, or a plain fixed account. They don't pay much, usually 5 percent to 7 percent, but there's no risk of losing your principal, either.

Balanced

These funds made up of a combination of stocks and bonds. This gives you what some would call "the best of both worlds." You've got some stability with the bonds, but the opportunity to grow with the stocks. They are not as stable as the guaranteed accounts, but they will give you a better return. They are not as volatile as stock funds, but will give you a lower return.

Growth accounts

These are the equity (stock market) accounts that do so well over time, but scare an awful lot of people. Review Chapter 6 on mutual funds and my discussion on the stock market from a historical perspective. And keep in mind that historically, the stock market has gone up in 70 percent of the years.

Your company stock

You may work for a publicly held company and can purchase your company's stock in your retirement plan. You must be careful, however. While we have all heard stories about all the millionaires created at Microsoft, it can be very dangerous to put a big chunk of your retirement funds in one stock. Many companies use their own stock for the matching part of their contributions. This should be enough exposure to one stock for you. You know your company better than I do. Just be careful and don't get carried away.

Asset class performance

Let's review the average annual rate of return for these asset classes.

Asset Class	5 years	10 years	15 years	20 years
Balanced	12.43	12.38	13.12	13.05
Growth	14.93	14.62	13.95	17.14
Equity Income	16.71	15.05	14.72	14.55
Agrees. Growth	15.82	15.96	13.50	15.59
International	11.44	6.27	14.91	14.05
Fixed	6.39	8.13	9.18	9.40

Source: CDA/Wiesenberger. Period through December 31, 1997

You'll remember from Chapter 4 the importance of understanding how compound interest can work for you. This really makes a difference when you are able to achieve higher rates of return. So as you look at these returns over the years, reflect on that discussion and recognize how much better off you will be with higher returns.

Allocation

Okay, now is the moment of truth. How do you invest *your* retirement dollars? One of the reasons companies hire me to provide retirement planning advice to their employees is that they don't want to assume the liability of advising their employees how to invest their money. It is something I really enjoy doing because I can really make a difference in a person's retirement security. Remember, my vision is to have a positive impact on others so they can enjoy a secure and happy retirement. I will do that by giving you the benefit of some of my knowledge to help you determine how to invest.

But not now! You'll have to wait until Chapter 13 for that information. Please understand that it is difficult to give you hard and fast rules concerning how to invest your retirement money. Your risk tolerance, your years until retirement, your future financial needs, your current financial needs differ from everyone else. Nevertheless, I will talk about specific allocation in Chapter 12.

Not participating

One final word about participating. I know I sound like a nag, but I talk to you from having the experience of meeting people who haven't prepared for their retirement.

Having a voluntary retirement plan is one of the greatest privileges and benefits you'll ever have. Yet most people fail to take full advantage of it. They are always waiting until they "have enough money" to invest. Face it, you will never have *enough*. However, if you don't participate, you won't have *anything* when you retire.

Again, it's a matter of priority. Most people choose to spend their money today rather than saving it for tomorrow. I know you can do both if you are careful in how you spend your money. If you follow my advice, the results will be gratifying and you will thank me in the end.

Chapter 11

Raiding your retirement: Certain financial death

I have told you that there are three factors that will determine how secure your retirement is: how much you invest; the return you get; and whether you leave it in or take it out along the way. I've spent loads of time talking about the first two; let's talk about the third.

I have met with lots of people who are retiring from the same company. They had the same exact plan. They worked approximately the same number of years. They put essentially the same amount into retirement. They made the same choices. But one had lots more money at retirement than the other. Any guess why? That's right. Because one person took money out of his plan along the way.

Withdrawing money

Many people look at their retirement plan as their personal banks. Anytime they are short on cash, they just rob the bank. And I know people tell you how great a 401(k) is because you can borrow money *from* it. As you will see shortly, that is hogwash, and I'm going to prove it to you.

The cost

Remember, everything you do has a financial cost. Taking money out of your retirement plan today costs you tomorrow. Before we look at the issue of borrowing from your retirement plan, let's first look at the cost of withdrawing money from your plan.

Let's look at the situation of two people I recently met at a preretirement seminar I did for a major corporation. I'm going to change the facts somewhat for simplicity and to make sure they are unrecognizable. I'll call them John and Tom. Each has worked for the same company for 35 years. They've each put away $120 per month in their retirement plans and averaged an 11-percent rate of return.

However, when I sat down to give them some ideas for maximizing their retirement security, I looked at their retirement statements and saw one startling difference: *John had $492,829 and Tom only had $218,761!* How could this have been? Didn't they do everything identically? Well, as it turns out, they did not.

Tom robbed the bank

Twenty years ago, when the rules were different, Tom withdrew $30,000 from his plan. Remember, everything has a cost. *Tom's cost of taking out $30,000 was more than $268,000!* And that's only up to now. It's one thing to have $268,000 less, but wait until you see the impact of that over the rest of his life!

Because Tom chose to take $30,000 from his plan 20 years ago, he has more than *one-quarter of a million dollars less* today. When I discussed this with Tom, he had a tough time remembering what he did with the $30,000. Oh, he had some credit card loans, and a car loan or two. But it certainly wasn't worth losing $250,000 over.

His only comment was, "I guess I thought the money was important to me at the time. I never thought about the consequences of taking that money out. If I had known, I would have never done it. And if I knew then what I know now, I wouldn't have charged so much on my credit cards in the first place."

Learn from Tom's mistake

The key here is to learn from Tom's mistakes. He said "If I knew then what I know now." Now that you've heard about what happened to Tom, you won't have to make that same mistake.

Earlier in the book, I told you about the clients who came in my office "needing" $16,000 from their retirement plan. When I explained the consequences, when I told them about Tom, they decided they could live without the money. I always tell my clients that it's cheaper to learn from other people's mistakes than from their own!

I realize that there are emergencies that may cause a financial crunch. And sometimes, taking money out of a retirement plan is literally a matter of life and death. But most times it's not. Most times it's just to support a life style that has gotten out of hand. It's to pay for that "stuff" you have accumulated. Life's not about accumulating stuff; life's about enjoying your time here and hopefully making a difference.

Borrowing from your plan

I can hear it now. "But I'm only borrowing from myself —and I'm paying myself interest, which is better than borrowing from the bank." Better, yes. Good, no.

Many people will say that I am wrong, that borrowing is a good deal. I discussed earlier, you can borrow up to 50 percent of your account, up to $50,000, with up to five years to repay. I'm going to show you why borrowing isn't such a good deal after all.

You aren't really borrowing

Here's where the confusion starts. You aren't really borrowing, no matter what you are told. You can't borrow money from yourself. You can borrow from the bank. You can borrow from the credit union. You can borrow from the mortgage company. You can't borrow from yourself.

This is the same silly game banks play when you make a passbook loan. You "borrow" the money from your retirement account. Therefore, you've reduced your assets in your retirement account. Instead of $60,000, you now have $30,000. But you have $30,000 more in your checking account. That is not a loan. You are simply taking the money out of your right pocket and putting it into your left pocket.

Lose the growth

And, by the way, what about the money you had invested in that growth account? When you "borrow" your money, what do you think happens to the value of that account? Two things: First, it is reduced by the amount you "borrow." Second, it stops earning money for you.

The IRS might call it a loan; the plan may call it a loan; but it's really not. It is a withdrawal that is not taxed, and that's all it is.

Not paying yourself interest

Here's a shocker for the "but I am paying myself interest" crowd. You're not paying yourself interest. Just like you can't borrow from yourself, you can't pay yourself interest. You can return your money and a little bit extra, but that extra is not really interest because you haven't earned any more money. Again, you're just taking it from one pocket and putting it into the other.

Stop making contributions

Another problem is that many people, when paying back their loan, stop making contributions to their 401(k). In other words, they use the money that they had previously been contributing to the plan to repay the loan. So what is happening is that you are losing the growth on what would have been up to five years of contributions. That can have a devastating effect on your retirement.

Plus the taxes on the payback

So now you've taken money out of your retirement plan. You're not making any money on that money, and now you have to pay it back. But, and this is a biggie, you have to pay it back after you've paid income taxes on the money you've earned to pay it back. Sound confusing? Let me explain. It is important to understand this because this practice makes a bad deal even worse.

You borrow $20,000. You have to repay that $20,000 plus "interest." Forget the interest for a minute. You have to repay $20,000. Where does this $20,000 come from? It comes from your earnings. But the $20,000 you pay back is not tax-deductible. So you have to come up with the $20,000 after taxes. If you remember our discussion on taxes, that means you have to earn $30,000 to be left with $20,000. And guess what happens when you eventually take that $20,000 out of your retirement plan? Bingo. You'll pay taxes again on that same money. What a deal. You've paid taxes twice on the same money. No wonder the government lets you "borrow" your money. It's a tax bonanza!

If you leave your company

The other factor that could actually impact your career is that if you leave your employer for whatever reason— new opportunity, layoff, you quit— then the loan must be paid back within two months. This really can put a crimp in your plans.

What if you are offered a job and you have a loan against your 401(k)? You loan is due within 60 days. That means that if you don't have the money, or don't want to have to declare the loan as a premature distribution (subject to taxes and penalties), you can't take the new job, unless your new employer allows you to transfer the loan to the new plan.

The ultimate cost

The ultimate effect of borrowing from your retirement account, as we saw in our discussion of Tom and John, is that you'll have potentially hundreds of thousands of dollars less at retirement. But what does that really mean to you? Let's take a further look at Tom and John. To make the comparison meaningful, I'm going to make some generalizations: both men are 60 years old; both will begin receiving Social Security at age 62; both are married and the wives are 57 years old; and both need $3,000 per month to live. Remember the one big difference: *John has $492,829 in his retirement plan; Tom has only $218,761.*

The following chart shows the type of analysis I run for my clients. It gives them (and me) an idea as to whether they have enough to retire in the style that they desire.

Let me explain the analysis to you. This is a little more complicated than the analysis I prepare for my clients for one simple reason: In this chart, I am comparing two people. For illustration purposes, I want you to see the consequences of Tom withdrawing $30,000 from his plan.

Age	Living Expenses	Social Security	Tom's $218,761 @6%	John's $492,829 @6%	Tom's $218,761 @9%	John's $492,829 @9%
60	3,000	0	194,727	485,289	200,718	499,452
61	3,120	0	167,765	475,708	179,541	505,161
62	3,245	936	149,229	475,648	166,658	521,584
63	3,375	964	128,321	474,326	151,335	538,205
64	3,510	1,489	110,993	477,758	139,543	561,230
65	3,650	1,534	91,440	480,211	125,485	585,125
66	3,796	1,580	69,475	481,572	108,905	609,912
67	3,948	1,627	44,898	481,721	89,518	635,616
68	4,106	1,676	17,496	480,528	67,015	662,261
69	4,270	1,726	0	477,852	41,053	689,872
70	4,441	1,778	0	473,541	11,258	718,470
75	5,403	2,061	0	421,285	0	877,040
80	6,573	2,389	0	297,568	0	1,063,177
85	7,998	2,770	0	65,333	0	1,277,866
90	9,730	3,211	0	0	0	1,519,408

The first column shows their ages. Column two reflects their living expenses. They need $3,000 to live today. I am assuming a 4-percent inflation rate. Therefore, their income needs go up by 4 percent each year. Column three is their Social Security income. John's and Tom's benefits begin three years before their wives' because they are three years older. Columns 4, 5, 6, and 7 show how much each family will have left of their original retirement amount depending on whether they earn 6 percent on their money or 9 percent on their money.

The results

It doesn't take a brain surgeon to see the results of Tom's early withdraw of $30,000. Given his desire for an income of $3,000 per month, he will run out of money at age 68 if he earns 6 percent on his retirement funds, and age 70 if he earns 9 percent. Compare that to John's. Remember, John left all his money in his plan for his retirement. If he earns 6 percent on his money, he will make it to age 85. The chart doesn't reflect it, but if he earns 9 percent, he will make it to age 128! Quite a difference, wouldn't you say?

The question Tom asked me was, "What can I do to make my money last longer?" Well, I told him he could try to go for a higher rate of return on his money, but that wasn't reasonable or realistic given that he didn't want to take too much risk at his age. So his only choice was to either get a part-time job or reduce his standard of living. How much would he have to reduce his living expenses? I'm glad you asked.

If he cuts his family income to $2,000, he will have enough until age 82 if he earns 6 percent, and to age 100 if he earns 9 percent. So by cutting his income and increasing his risk, he stands a chance of having enough until age 85 to 90. By the way, this is $2,000 before taxes. It doesn't leave a whole lot to live on when you take out taxes. It's certainly not what he had worked his whole life for, but it's the price he will pay for robbing his retirement fund.

Now do you believe me?

I hope you now understand why I keep harping on the terror of withdrawing money from your retirement plan. I know that when you're young, it's hard to worry about retirement. You have house payments, college expenses, clothing expenses for the kids, just to name a few. But understand that you can still enjoy your life without having to mortgage your retirement. If you think it's tough living on a budget while you're raising a family, just wait until you're retired and you want to finally have time to enjoy yourself and your grandchildren—but you won't if you spend all your retirement money while you are young. I have seen poor retirees, and it's not a pretty picture. That's why I'm dedicating so much of my life to making sure this doesn't happen to you and other hard-working Americans.

Part II

Your Secure Retirement

Chapter 12

Investing your retirement money

Okay, this is where the rubber meets the road. This is the point where it is time to *properly*, and I emphasize the word properly, invest your retirement money. Statistics show that one of the most common reasons people don't accumulate enough money in their retirement plans is because they haven't invested it properly. That means they have been too conservative in their choices. We have talked about stock market risks again and again, and I hope you understand the value of long-term investing in the best companies in the world and the importance of achieving higher returns on your money.

So, the question is, "Exactly how do I invest my retirement money? Where should I put it?" The chart at the end of this chapter contains my recommended allocation based on your risk tolerance.

Your risk tolerance

In my practice, I use a combination of a scoring system and personal interviews to determine my clients' risk tolerance. That's because:

1. Neither one by itself is an accurate indication of risk tolerance.

2. Determining risk tolerance is not an exact science.

During a raging bull market, there is no such thing as too much risk. Everything is going up. Excessive risk doesn't hurt you. In fact, you are rewarded for it.

However, when the market heads down, it's payback time! If you've turned your back on risk, if you've invested everything for growth, you'll get your head handed to you.

One of my jobs as a personal financial advisor is to match my clients' investment portfolio with their risk tolerance. Because most of my clients are retired, I don't want their life style to suffer in a market drop. So we don't invest for the highest rate of return, we invest for the highest rate of return *given their risk tolerance*. Those last four words are very important, and that understanding is what separates professional advisors from pretend advisors. It's what separates professional advisors from the magazines touting the best funds. It's what separates professional advisors from mutual funds advertising their great rates of return.

Most people today have an unrealistic expectation as to what to expect from the stock market. Since the market crash in 1987, the returns have been phenomenal, even with the drop in 1998. They are also unsustainable. In other words, this is going to end someday. And when it does, I don't want my clients' life styles to suffer.

When you're young, stock market drops aren't a problem. On the contrary, they're an advantage. They allow you to buy the greatest companies in the world "on sale." However, once you've retired, any advantage of a market drop is gone. That's why I invest my retired clients' money more conservatively than I do that of working folks.

With that in mind, let's look at my description of what I consider the five risk profiles:

1. Conservative.

2. Moderately conservative.

3. Moderate.

4. Moderately aggressive.

5. Aggressive.

Conservative

If you are conservative, you feel most comfortable with all of your money in guaranteed accounts, no matter what. You believe that the stock market is too high and it will soon come tumbling down, and stay down. (Of course, you also thought that when the Dow Jones Industrial Average was at 2,000!) You are satisfied with your money in the bank even though you are receiving a very low rate of return. You are not willing to do anything that involves risk to increase your rate of return.

You either lived through the depression or were close to someone who did, and you bought into the argument that another depression is going to happen...soon. You think the stock market is a casino and you don't want to take all that risk.

You might, however, invest in government or tax-free bonds, not realizing that there's loads of volatility in long-term bonds. Nevertheless, if it isn't guaranteed in some form or fashion, you don't want to consider it.

There's nothing wrong with this strategy if you are already retired with enough income to last the rest of your life. However, if you are under 65 or don't have sufficient funds, you'll probably come up short.

Moderately conservative

If you are moderately conservative, you are not too comfortable with the stock market as a place for your money. You've heard stories about people losing money, and don't want to take that risk. You feel most comfortable with your money in the bank. You are willing to accept a relatively low rate of return in exchange for the security of knowing your accounts will not fluctuate in value.

On the other hand, you do recognize that the stock market is a place for some of your money. You know that money in the bank just isn't going to cut it. It scares the heck out of you, but you are willing to close your eyes, hold your nose, and put some of your money in stocks.

Moderate

If you are moderate, you are a middle-of-the-roader. You are, in fact, my average client. You want higher returns and are willing to take some measured risk to achieve them. You understand that the stock market is volatile, and while not real comfortable with it, you are willing to live through temporary declines to participate in the permanent increases.

You recognize that you cannot retire in the lifestyle you desire by accepting rates of return offered by fixed investments. You cringe every time the market goes down, and you get scared when you read doom and gloom headlines, but you grit your teeth and try to ignore what's going on. You probably even avoid looking at your fund statements.

Moderately aggressive

If you fall into the moderately aggressive category, you realize that the stock market is the place to be long-term, and you feel comfortable with that. You look at dips in the market as opportunities to buy stock in the greatest companies in the world while they're on sale. You don't care about the fluctuations in the market, because your goal is to accumulate shares of the companies or mutual funds you like. And given the choice, you'd rather pay lower prices than higher prices.

You have confidence in the long-range outlook in the market. You feel the market will be higher in 20 years than it is today, so you're not that concerned with what happens in the meantime.

Nevertheless, you do get a bit concerned every time the market takes a big drop, because all you read about and hear on the news is how bad things are going to get. Maybe they are right for the first time ever...maybe the sky *is* falling.

But you regain your senses and think that if these companies were a good buy at higher prices, they can only be a better buy at lower prices. You keep your focus on what you are trying to accomplish long term, and you don't worry about the short term. You realize that because you are not liquidating 100 percent of your portfolio today or next month, or next year, it doesn't matter what the stock market does in the short run.

On the other hand, you are not so gung-ho that you would mortgage your house and throw it into the market. You realize that there are short-term risks, and that the only money that should be in the market are those funds that you won't need over the next few years.

Aggressive

If you are strongly aggressive, you love the action that the stock market brings. In fact, you think that investing in the stock market the traditional way is too boring and conservative. You buy stock on margin because you want to go for the gold. You think buying options is the way to go. You stay glued to CNBC and jump on any tip you can.

You've been spoiled by the last hot stock market and you don't think it will go down. You like listening to the gurus who tell you what's going to happen next.

You think that you can strike it rich in the investment arena. You've got a system that is going to make you rich. You'll even try commodities (heating oil, soybeans, etc.), or you'll buy options on stocks hoping you're right.

In effect, you'll lose lots of money (or miss out on making money) trying to get rich. And you will end up exactly where you didn't want to be.

Of course, there is always the chance that you're smarter than everyone else and you can beat the system. If not, you'll go down trying.

How you might invest

See which of my descriptions fits you best. The following chart shows my recommendation for long-term money based on your investment tolerance. Understand that this is just a generalization. I don't know you personally, so I can't make hard and fast decisions for you.

It is very possible that you will change from one category to another as you get older. You might start out moderately aggressive and work your way over toward the moderate category. Times change, and so do we.

To make it simple, I have broken the choices down into two:

- **Fixed (F)**—These include the fixed account in your retirement plan plus bank accounts and any government and tax-free bonds. However, remember our discussion about how bonds fluctuate. The best way to make bonds a safer investment is to invest in short-term (two- to five-year) bonds.

- **Stock (S)**—These are the mutual funds outside your plan and the equity choices inside.

Age	Conservative		Moderately Conservative		Moderate		Moderately Aggressive		Aggressive	
	F	S	F	S	F	S	F	S	F	S
20s	0	100	0	100	0	100	0	100	0	100
30s	20	80	10	90	0	100	0	100	0	100
40s	40	60	30	70	20	80	10	90	0	100
50s	60	40	50	50	30	70	20	80	10	90
60s	80	20	60	40	50	50	40	60	20	80
70+	100	0	70	30	60	40	50	50	30	70

Diversification

One further thought before you make your investment decisions: There is a way to further reduce risk in each of the two categories, and that is through diversification. Just because you determine that you should be 70 percent invested in stocks doesn't mean just one type of stock. Remember our discussion of mutual funds? There are a number of different categories of mutual funds. In addition, there are several styles, such as value investing and growth investing. There are large-cap funds (those that invest in big companies), and small-cap funds.

In addition, you need to consider investing a portion of your money internationally. Personally, I don't think that if you are in your 20s or 30s, international investing is that important. Studies show that international investing reduces risk by spreading your investment across the globe. The concept is that different markets do better at different times. We never really know which market is going to perform the best going forward; that's why we diversify.

So as you get closer to retirement, you need to further diversify your investment across different classes of equity funds, and different countries. All this works toward reducing risk.

Chapter 13

Determining your retirement savings needs

The next question is, "How much do I need to put away for my retirement?" This is a tough one to answer because there are so many uncertainties.

When you are planning for your retirement, your goal is to have the largest lump sum possible. In the old days, corporations provided monthly retirement income to their retirees. Now, with 401(k)s, etc., it is up to you to grow your own pot of money.

Assumptions

The amount of money you will need at retirement is based on a number of assumptions. Let's look at the factors that will determine whether or not you can afford to retire the way you desire.

Your age at retirement

You must decide when you want to retire. The earlier you retire, the larger the lump sum of money you're going to need simply because you will have more years to live without a salary. Retiring at 55 sounds nice, but it turns out to be a burden if you haven't planned properly.

Waiting five years to retire makes things much easier for you because:

1. You have five years longer to grow your current assets.

2. You have five years longer to invest new money.

3. You have five years less that you need to depend on your retirement money.

Your desired monthly income

How much income will you need each month? When making that decision, be sure to take into consideration any debts and unusual expenses you may no longer have. For example, if you've paid off your home and have no college expenses, then your cost of living will be significantly lower.

Determine an amount that you will need as monthly income based on today's dollars. In other words, if you retired today, and assuming you were debt free (or close), how much income would you need each month?

The rate of inflation

Once you have determined your desired monthly income, you must adjust it for inflation. Today, I'm using 4 percent as the rate of inflation. That means that if you're 45 years old and need $3,000 a month if you retire today, you will actually need $5,400 if you retire at age 60.

Inflation is the one factor that people tend to ignore. They think that once they retire, rising prices won't affect them. But just ask current retirees about the cost of health care and other expenses. Inflation doesn't stop just because you've decided to retire.

Social Security

Are you going to include Social Security in your calculations? If you are in your 50s or older, that should be no problem. If you are younger, it would be more prudent not to include it.

Call (800) 772-1213 and ask for the *Request for Personal Earnings and Benefit Estimate Statement* from the Social Security Administration. This will give you an idea what your benefits will be.

Monthly investments

How much will you be investing monthly in your retirement plan or elsewhere between now and the day you retire? As you know by now, this will have an enormous impact on the amount you have available upon retirement.

One of the things that makes this component so difficult is that the money you have available for investment should go up each year as your income increases. Nevertheless, come up with a figure you are comfortable with.

Rate of growth

Obviously you don't know how fast your money will grow between now and the day you die, but you must make some assumptions. While you're putting money into your retirement plan or mutual fund, you can assume 10 percent per year if you are investing in the growth accounts. A lot of people have been spoiled by the great stock market returns of recent years and have been assuming 15 percent or more. Don't do that; it's not going to happen over time. If you have money in the bank or in the fixed accounts in your retirement plan, then use 5 to 6 percent.

One last point about assumptions. When working with clients, I always assume that if things are going to fall one way or the other, they are going to fall to the negative side. In other words, I like to plan for the worst. Planning for the best is just wishful thinking.

I'm not a negative person, far from it. I just believe that you will get into trouble thinking you're going to get every break from now to the day you die. Emergencies will crop up. There will be drops in the stock market. You might not earn as much as you want. You might lose your job. You might want to be able to give away some money during retirement. You might live longer than you expect. Remember, we are going for retirement security, which really means peace of mind. That means not having to worry that something might throw you into financial turmoil. That's what planning is all about. So if I'm going to err, I err on the side of conservatism.

Life expectancy

I've got a great question for you: How long are you going to live? No idea, right? Right. But you have to make some assumptions, because your needs are going to be a lot different if you live to age 95 instead of age 75.

With life expectancy as it is today, I like to use ages 95 to 100. Now, you're going to say, "But I won't live that long." If you are sure of that, then use a lower age. Just don't blame me if you run out of money early!

Calculation

You can see that this is a lot of information. That's why I use a number of computer programs when working with clients. However, I will give you a basic format that will let you determine your own needs. Remember, what we are trying to determine is how much you must put away each month to retire with a specified amount of money.

Please understand one thing before you rely on this for your retirement: *Don't!* It is such a broad generalization that it might get you fairly close, but there are too many individual factors that need to be part of the equation to rely on it solely.

I include this in the book only because you might want to get a rough idea where you stand. For more accurate numbers, retirement planning software is really needed. There are several mutual fund companies, such as Vanguard and T. Rowe Price, that have software available, as well as most financial planners. I would recommend one of those two routes.

Meanwhile, let's walk through the form as I explain each line.

1. Annual income in today's dollars   _____

2. Annual income in inflated dollars
   (Multiply #1 by **inflation rate**)   _____

3. Social Security/Pension Income   _____

4. Annual Income Shortfall
   (Subtract #3 from #2)   _____

5. Lump sum needed (Divide # 4 by .05%)   _____

6. Current Savings/Investments   _____

7. Future value of Current Savings
   (Multiply #6 by **growth rate**)   _____

8. Lump sum still needed.
   (Subtract #7 from #5)   _____

9. Divide #8 by $10,000   _____

10. Monthly savings required
    (Multiply #9 by **monthly rate**)   _____

Years to retirement	5 yrs.	10 yrs.	15 yrs.	20 yrs.	25 yrs.
4% inflation rate	1.22	1.48	1.80	2.19	2.67
7% growth rate	1.40	1.97	2.76	3.87	5.42
10% growth rate	1.61	2.59	4.17	6.72	10.83
7% monthly rate	140	58	31	19	12
10% monthly rate	129	49	24	13	8

1. Enter the amount of annual income you would need today if you retired. Hopefully, you will be debt-free when you retire, so be sure to take that into consideration.

2. We need to inflate that income because the cost of living is going to go up over the years. On the table, find the inflation rate that coincides with your years to retirement. That first line is the multiplier for a 4 percent inflation rate.

3. Enter the annual amount you expect in the form of Social Security and any pensions to which you are entitled.

4. Subtract line 3 from 2, and you will see the income shortfall you will face.

5. Divide that shortfall by .05. That will give you an approximate lump sum of money you will need to generate sufficient income to make up for that shortfall.

6. Enter your current savings and investments in banks, mutual funds, and retirement plans.

7. Multiply that figure by one of the growth rates on the next two lines of the table. I have given you the choice of a 7 percent growth rate or a 10 percent growth rate.

8. Subtract line 7 from line 5, and you will see the lump sum you still need to accumulate for retirement.

9. Divide that figure by $10,000.

10. Finally, go back to the box and find the corresponding monthly rate, again choosing between 7 and 10 percent. Multiply that number by the figure in line 9. That gives you the monthly amount you must invest.

Calculating retirement needs is not a perfect science by any means. One of the problems is that you get a monthly investment amount that must be made every month from here on out until retirement. If retirement is 20 years away, that is going to be too high for you now. But as time goes on, it should get easier because your income will go up.

The key is to keep close tabs on your progress and make adjustments to your investments and your portfolio as you get closer to retirement.

Chapter 14

If you are retiring in 20 to 25 years

If you fall into this category, you're lucky. You've got all the time in the world to plan for a secure retirement. You've got all the options available to you. All it takes is the desire to make smart decisions from this point forward.

Hopefully, you've digested all the information I've presented so far and you're ready to move forward. Remember, achieving retirement is simple, but it's not easy. You have to restrain yourself from following the herd and making stupid decisions.

Your vision

As I said in the beginning of this book, everything happens twice: once in your mind and once in reality. You've got the liberty of time to plan your vision, and better yet, to fulfill it. Take the time to decide exactly what you want to accomplish between now and the day you retire. You will be pleasantly surprised that these dreams really can and do come true.

Your retirement plan

If you work for an employer who offers any type of retirement plan (401(k), tax-sheltered annuity, deferred compensation, etc.), take full advantage of it. Put as much as you can into your plan, and invest it all in growth funds.

Remember, you aren't only investing until the day you retire, you're investing until the day you die. Hopefully, that will be a long, long time. And by now you know you will get the best returns over the long term by investing in equities—the growth funds in your retirement plan. So put all your money there.

If you're self-employed, take advantage of the retirement plans available to you: SEP, SIMPLE, IRA, Keogh. Put as much as you can every month into growth mutual funds.

Take advantage of the Roth IRA. This money is not deductible, but grows tax-free and is not taxable when you withdraw it. It's the best plan available today.

Life insurance

If you have children or dependents, buy the cheapest term insurance you can from a solid insurance company. The company should be rated at least A+ by A.M. Best *and* at least AA by Standard & Poor's.

Get 20- or 30-year level premium/level death benefit. Don't worry about accumulating cash values. This is not the place to do it. Term insurance will give you the cheapest coverage, your mutual funds or retirement plans will provide the savings growth.

Your home

Your home is not an investment, your home is a place to live. Don't buy/build an expensive home thinking you'll make lots of money when you sell it. People who say that their home is the *best* investment they ever made are people whose home is the *only* investment they ever made!

Be practical. Get a nice home in a good neighborhood, but don't pour lots of money into it. That money should go into your retirement plan.

Credit cards

Don't carry credit card balances, especially if the rate is above 12 percent. You are making money for the credit card company at a terrible cost to you. If you have high-interest cards, pay them off. It is the best use of your money.

I like people to use the American Express Green Card because you can't carry a balance—you have to pay it off in 30 days. Of course, you have to pay $35 a year for that card. But it's a small price to pay if it gives you the discipline not to carry a balance. It will save you thousands in interest charges.

Cars

Don't buy new cars. Buy two-year-old cars still under warranty. It will save you tens of thousands of dollars between now and the time you retire.

Outside investments

Once you've maxed out your company retirement plan and contributed to a Roth IRA, then start an outside mutual fund. You can make monthly contributions as small as $25. Like your retirement plan, you want growth funds, not bond funds. You should be shooting for maximum growth at this point in your life.

Check out the "tax-managed" mutual funds that specialize in producing high *after-tax* results. Don't confuse these with "tax-free" bond funds. Tax-managed growth funds have low turnover and pay particular attention to the tax ramifications of their activities. Their goal is to give you growth without creating lots of capital gains along the way. You will, of course, pay taxes on your gains when you sell shares in the fund.

College expenses

You are probably thinking about educating your children. It will certainly be easier for you if you have the money already saved for their education. There are two ways to do this.

To start, you can put money into a custodial account. The first $700 (1998 figures) of income will be tax free if the children are under the age of 14. The next $700 will be taxed at their income-tax rate, while everything above $1,400 will be taxed at your rate. If the children are 14 or older, all income will be taxed at their rate. That's the advantage. The disadvantage is that the money becomes theirs at age 18 or 21, even if they don't go to college. If they can qualify for scholarships, this money will count against them.

The second way to save for college is to put the money in your name and earmark it for your children's education. The disadvantage is that you will be responsible for the taxes. However, if you use a tax-managed fund, then taxes should not be a big problem. Once your children need the money, you can transfer shares to them and they can pay the capital gains taxes. The advantage here is two-fold. If your child doesn't go to college, you can keep the money. If your child does go to college, this money will count less against them when they try to qualify for financial aid or scholarship.

The money should be invested in growth mutual funds when the children are younger. As they get within several years of college, you might want to start moving it into more conservative investments.

Chapter 15

If you are retiring in 15 years

At this point, you've still got plenty of time to make good decisions. Hopefully you've learned from any mistakes and from now on will concentrate on doing only that which will help you reach your long-term goals.

Your vision

Speaking of long-term goals, if you really don't have them firmly established, go ahead and do it now. You've got 15 years to go. It's a lot of time, but it will fly by. Where did the last 15 years go? The next 15 will go by even faster.

When do you want to retire? What will you need in the form of income? What about college education for your children? Will it put a crimp in your retirement plans? Will you be debt-free by the time you retire (and, hopefully, long before)? Are you putting enough in your retirement plan? Are you making the right choices? Let's talk.

Your retirement plan

You still have lots of time ahead, but you've got lots of things to do. The next 15 years can make or break you.

You must put away the maximum amount you can. You must be invested primarily in the growth accounts. Look at the retirement savings calculator in Chapter 14, or get a program from one of the mutual fund companies. See if you're on track. It might be possible that you need to invest more than your retirement plan allows. If so, go to an outside mutual fund.

If you're self-employed, there are a number of plans available, such as the SEP, SIMPLE, IRA, and Keogh. The Roth IRA is a great idea for you.

Life insurance

Term insurance is the way to go for the most coverage at the lowest price. Get a 20- or 30-year term policy, with a guaranteed premium and a guaranteed death benefit. That means that while the policy is in force, the premium can't go up and the death benefit is guaranteed not to go down. Choose only those companies rated A+ by A.M. Best *and* AA or better by Standard and Poor's. Don't get caught up in the "whole life" argument. There are better places to accumulate money, such as a Roth IRA and your retirement plan at work.

Your home

Have you thought about what you are going to do? Maybe downsize in several years? Or, heaven forbid, upsize? In any case, work to be mortgage-free by the time you retire. Again, you can do this one of two ways: Pay extra on your mortgage or put that extra in a mutual fund.

Credit cards

I hope you know by now what a waste credit card interest is. You've probably paid enough to know that it's the road to financial oblivion. You don't carry a balance. And don't finance large purchases; put them off until you can afford them. At this point in your life, every financial decision is going to have a major impact. Bad decisions will lead to bad results.

Cars

Hopefully you've outgrown the need for new cars. They're such a waste of money. Heck, it's a used car once you sign the paperwork, even before you drive it off the lot! So buy a two-year-old car still under factory warranty.

Outside investments

If you've maxed your retirement contributions, then invest additional money in outside investments, either individual stocks or mutual funds. Tax-managed funds are a good idea because they can give you growth without creating a big capital gains problem.

College expenses

College expenses present a real problem for people within 15 years of retirement. Do you use your retirement money for the kids' education, or do you try to pay for it out of income?

I prefer the latter. This might sound selfish, but don't jeopardize your retirement to pay for college. There are loans and scholarships out there for anyone who wants to go to college. Student loan programs and work/loan programs are available. Take advantage of them.

Chapter 16

If you are retiring in 10 years

It's getting closer! You can almost see that light at the end of that long, long tunnel. But there's still a lot of work to be done.

The next 10 years will fly by. You won't know what happened to them, just like you don't know what happened to the last 10, or 20 for that matter. You still have time, but it's going to be tougher if you haven't yet started to plan.

Your vision

Okay, it's time to make some real decisions here. When are you going to retire? How much monthly income will you need? Is there enough time to accumulate it? If not, what are you going to do? Keep working? Get a part-time job? Cut back on your living expenses? These are just a few decisions you face.

You need to get focused in your mind exactly what you want to accomplish in the next 10 years. Then you should sit down and create a timetable for each of those actions. Let's look at them.

Your retirement plan

Hopefully, you're taking advantage of available retirement plans. You're putting the maximum in. You're investing them in the right fashion. Review my allocation recommendations in Chapter 13 to see where you should be.

You might want to be more conservative if you've been ultra-aggressive. Conversely, you might want to increase your risk if you've been ultra-conservative. The retirement calculator in Chapter 13 should help you see where you are and where you need to go.

If you are self-employed, plow all the money you can into the various plans available. The Keogh allows the most. Or you can do a SEP, SIMPLE, or an IRA. The Roth IRA still makes sense at your age. The money has to stay in five years, and you have 10 to go.

Life insurance

Term insurance is the way to go to get the most coverage for the least money. Make sure the company is rated at least A+ by A.M. Best *and* AA by Standard & Poor's. Get a 20-year level premium/level policy.

Your home

As I've said many times, retirement is a lot easier and more secure without a house payment. At this point in your life, it would be nice to know that no matter what happens, you have a paid-for home. Make it a specific goal to pay off your home.

Credit cards

I don't have to tell you what a waste of money credit card interest is. If you been receiving all those unsolicited credit card applications, you know what a great business it is...for them! For you, it is bad news if you carry a balance.

Get your credit cards paid off as soon as possible. And from now on, don't use them unless you make the full payment the next month.

Cars

Cars are a means of transportation, not a trophy of your success (or ability to get credit). Buy only two-year-old or older used cars still under warranty. There are some great buys out there, and the cars run like new.

Outside investments

Invest any money not in retirement accounts in mutual funds that fit your risk tolerance as I discussed in Chapter 12. Consider either tax-managed mutual funds or tax-deferred annuities.

The advantage of the former is that they are managed to reduce income taxes. The advantage of the latter is that they have a death benefit that can protect your spouse in the event of your death. I have found that husbands who have pensions appreciate the death protection for their wives, especially if there will be no pension benefits for the surviving spouse. The disadvantage of annuities is that the money must stay in until age 59½ to avoid a 10-percent IRS penalty, the fees tend to be a bit high on some of the plans, and the money comes out in the form of ordinary income as opposed to capital gains. However, in addition to the death benefit protection (which may or may not be important to you), you can currently switch between the different growth accounts without any tax liability. This provision, however, could change some day.

College expenses

If you have children in college, don't take your retirement money to pay for it (unless you have plenty of money). There are plenty of grants and student loans available. Although it sounds selfish, I have seen too many people create financial disaster for themselves by taking everything to pay for their kids education. After all, if you use everything to pay for education, who's going to support you during your retirement?

Chapter 17

If you are retiring in 5 years

Time is running out! You're going to have to make some tough decisions. So let's get going.

Your vision

Exactly what do you want to have accomplished by the day you retire? What about paying off your house? Your debts? Where are you going to live? How much will it take? Do you want to travel? Retire to another state?

Think about all these things and more. Develop a plan as to what you want your life to look like in five years. How are you going to spend your retirement years?

Your retirement plan

You might want to start moving from the more aggressive funds to the more moderate. Check your risk profile. Remember, even though you're retiring in five years, you still have many years to go. Invest for the rest of your life, not for the next five years.

The Roth IRA is a good plan for you. You have five years until retirement, and that is the length of time you must leave money in a Roth before you can take it out. Again, go for some growth.

Life insurance

Life insurance is getting more expensive. As a rule, I am a believer in term insurance. However, there are two exceptions: for estate-planning purposes, and as an alternative to a single-life annuity.

If you are going to receive a retirement annuity (as opposed to a lump-sum payout), it might make sense to explore the single-life option (as opposed to the survivor option) and buy a life insurance to take care of your spouse in the event of your death.

Understand that, contrary to what most insurance agents will tell you, my experience shows that this doesn't work in most cases. I've seen lots of people who have done this in the past and regret it today. That's because life insurance is not guaranteed, whereas a survivor annuity is. You need to be in good health, and the numbers have to work out with your employer. So, before you go ahead with this, check it out carefully.

Your home

My clients who are retired tell me that they appreciate having a house that is paid for. Not having to worry about house payments reduces stress and makes life a lot more enjoyable.

So in the next five years, work toward getting your home paid off, or at least having an equal amount in an outside mutual fund. Depending on how conservative you are, one of these choices will work out for you.

If you still have a substantial mortgage, check into refinancing. With mortgage interest rates currently at low levels, it's a good time to cut back on your payments. Then you can take the savings and use it to reduce your mortgage or put it into your retirement plan.

Credit cards

You are hopefully out of the spending mode by now. At this point, you do not want to have credit card debt anymore. Pay everything off in 30 days. You have to get used to living within your income.

Cars

Two-year-old used cars, still under warranty, are the best buys. I don't buy into the argument that you are "buying other people's problems" when you buy a used car. My wife and I have bought nothing but late-model used cars for years and have never had a problem. And we've saved lots of money!

Outside investments

Like your retirement plan funds, you might want to throttle back on the risk. Depending on your risk tolerance, you can move some money into fixed investments, or at least into growth-and-income funds.

You still need to be putting away money, however. Remember, the cost of living will continue to go up for the rest of your life. Therefore, you are going to need a good stream of income.

Use the retirement calculator in Chapter 13. This will give you an idea what kind of shape you will be in when you retire in five years. Hopefully, you won't need a part-time job.

College expenses

If you have kids in college, don't use your funds to pay for their education. If you do, you will be sacrificing your retirement. If you have funds saved for them, that's great. If not, there are plenty of loans and scholarships available.

Chapter 18

If you are retiring in 3 years

You're almost there. This is what you've been waiting for all these years. Will it be what you want? Let's find out.

Your vision

The type of retirement you have will be based on the choices you have made in the past. There's not a great deal that you can do at this point except really figure out what you want your life to be like starting in three years. Where do you want to live? What do you want to do? Will you retire somewhere else?

Your retirement plan

You might want to trim back your risk with retirement in three years. However, remember that you have to plan for the rest of your life, not just the next three years.

Check your risk profile in Chapter 12. Determine where you are most comfortable. But be careful about being too conservative. Remember, the cost of living will go up from today until the day you die, so you'll still need an increasing stream of income.

The Roth IRA makes sense even though you have to wait five years to take money out. Hopefully, you won't need it that soon.

Life insurance

If your company is going to pay you an annuity (as opposed to a lump sum), then you might want to consider taking the single-life and buying a life insurance policy. This decision depends on your age, health, and cost of taking a joint and survivor annuity.

This might be a bit early for you to know the numbers, but you can talk to someone at your company. If the monthly insurance premium is less than the amount you'd lose by taking the joint and survivor option instead of the single-life option, it might be worth your while. But remember, the life insurance premium isn't guaranteed, so you might run into a problem down the road.

Your home

My retired clients tell me they like having a paid-for home. At least if all else fails, they'll have a place to live. It makes sense for you to work really hard to get your home paid off.

Credit cards

Congratulations. You've outgrown your need for credit card debt! At least that's what I hope. If not, get out of debt, and soon.

Cars

Remember one thing: two-year-old used cars still under factory warranty. You don't need a fancy new car at this point in your life. You outgrew that need 30 years ago. By now you realize the expense of owning a new car.

Outside investments

Continue to put money into outside investments once you've funded your retirement plans and paid off your house. You will still need more money for retirement because of inflation.

Go to Chapter 13 and see how much you'll need to have in a lump sum to support your retirement life style. Then you'll know what you need to do.

College expenses

If this is still hanging over your head, don't use your retirement money. There are plenty of scholarships and loans available for kids who want to go to college. If you use your retirement money for college, you'll never recover from it. And you don't need the worry over who will support you after you retire.

Chapter 19

If you are retiring in 1 year

Your day is getting close. Now is the time to make some very important decisions.

Your vision

The next year will set the stage for your retirement. If you haven't already decided how you plan to live during your retirement, now is the time to do it.

Where do you want to live? How do you plan to spend your retirement? Are you going to travel? Spend time with family? Retire out-of-state?

Will you really retire, or continue to work? Part-time or full-time? Make sure you get this all clear in your mind so you can have a direction toward which to work.

Your retirement plan

What you do with your retirement plan will have a major impact on your retirement. There are three basic factors at work: how you are going to invest your money from this point forward; how much you are going to withdraw for monthly income; and when you are going to begin your withdrawals.

From an investment standpoint, realize that you can't make up for lost time by increasing your risk too much. While you probably have at least 25 years of retirement years ahead, you must plan realistically. Review my risk tolerance profile in Chapter 12. You will still need your money to grow, but you don't want to take undue risk at this point.

Obviously, the more income you take, the sooner you'll run out of money. Therefore, it's going to take some good planning to make sure you have sufficient funds to make it through your retirement.

You have a year to get it worked out. The decisions you are going to have to make will be many, but at least you've got some time. Let's discuss the decisions you'll be facing.

Form of retirement distribution

Many companies give you two choices on how you are going to get your retirement funds: in the form of a lump-sum distribution, or as monthly income. I have found that for almost everyone, receiving your distribution in the form of a lump sum offers some distinct advantages:

- You have access to that money in the event of an emergency.

- You can stop the income if you don't need it.

- If you die early, you can leave the balance to whomever you want.

Monthly annuity

If you chose the monthly income (called an annuity), you'll have the basic choice of having the income last during your life only or during the lifetime of you and your spouse. If you choose the latter, you will get a reduced income.

If there were only two choices, then it would be pretty simple. But many plans have a whole range of choices, varying the percentages all over the place: less now, more later; more now, less later; reduced 50 percent for your life and your spouse's; 75 percent for your life, 25 percent for your spouse's, etc. The choices can go on and on.

All in all, I only recommend the monthly annuity if you feel that you cannot possibly manage a lump sum. In other words, if you are sure that you would blow the money, or just couldn't possibly manage it, then choose the annuity option.

But remember the one big problem with the monthly annuity: Your income will not keep pace with the cost of living. What seems like a livable amount now might not be a livable amount in 15 years.

Lump sum

As I stated earlier, I recommend you take your retirement in the form of a lump-sum distribution. It gives you so many more choices. But you have to be careful, because Uncle Sam is waiting with his hand out. He wants your money! If you make one little mistake, it might cost you dearly. So let's look at the choices.

You will have to make decisions how to handle the lump-sum distribution from your retirement account. Your basic choices are:

- Leave it in the 401(k) (pension, profit-sharing, Keogh, etc.) plan at work.

- Transfer it to an IRA Rollover account. There will be no taxes withheld in a trustee-to-trustee transfer.

- Take it out in a lump sum and don't put it into an IRA Rollover. You will pay taxes, plus a 10 percent penalty if you are under the age of 55. Your employer will withhold 20 percent in taxes, but you'll still owe more.

- Take it out in a lump sum and, if you were born on or before January 1, 1936, you can qualify for special 10-year or five-year averaging. This is a way to have a reduced tax bite if you take your distribution in the form of a lump sum. That doesn't mean, by the way, that you pay the taxes over a period of time. You will pay all the taxes at once, just at a reduced tax rate.

If you roll it over

If you decide to roll over your retirement plan distribution, you have several choices, including a bank, brokerage firm, or mutual fund company. Assuming you recognize by now that you need a better rate of return than a bank will offer, then you need to decide whether you want to work by yourself or through a broker or investment advisor. Review Chapter 7 for a discussion of the choices. If you feel confident in your own abilities to manage your own finances, then by all means look to roll your retirement plan into no-load mutual funds.

However, if you don't have that confidence, you will want to seek out a financial advisor. Ideally, you will find someone who uses no-load funds (preferably institutional no load funds) and charges a fee rather than a commission.

Life insurance

If you are going to receive your retirement in the form of an annuity (monthly income), then you might want to consider taking the single-life option and purchase a life insurance policy to protect your spouse. However, this doesn't work in all situations. In fact, I have found that it doesn't work in most situations, contrary to what life insurance agents might lead you to believe.

Social Security

Now is the time to start preparing for Social Security. Review Chapter 8. Contact Social Security and see what month is best to claim benefits. It may be to your advantage to have your benefits begin in January, even though you don't plan on retiring until late in the year. Under current rules, many people can receive the most benefits possible with an application that is effective in January. Also, remember the special monthly rule that applies to your earnings for the first year of retirement.

Your home

It's tough to pay off a home in a one-year period of time, unless you owe very little. However, you should work to get it paid off as soon as possible. If you still have a rather large mortgage, then consider refinancing if you can cut about two percentage points off your current rate.

Credit cards

You don't want any credit card debt from this point forward. Things aren't going to get any better financially (in most situations), so don't spread out today's expenses over a period of time. Just charge what you can pay in full each month.

Cars

I know I sound like a broken record, but buy two-year-old cars still under factory warranty. Don't waste your money on new cars. It's a bad use of your funds.

Outside investments

You need to look at the risk you're taking in your outside investments. Again, review the risk tolerance chart in Chapter 12. You still need growth on your money because inflation is going to continue after you retire. Growth-and-income funds are a good place to move some funds.

Look at tax-advantaged funds if you plan to leave money in for the years ahead. Also, tax-deferred annuities might be a good place for some of the money you won't need because of the death benefit.

College expenses

Don't use your retirement funds for your children's education. It's too late and too dangerous for that now. Your retirement funds are for your retirement years. There are plenty of scholarships and loans available for college.

Chapter 20

If you are retiring tomorrow

Holy Cow! The day has arrived. Now what?

Your vision

Sit back, take a deep breath, and go to a quiet area. If you are married, both of you need to sit down and decide exactly what you want to happen now that you're ready to retire. Will you work part-time? Will your spouse continue to work? Will you move or stay where you are? Get a handle on what you want and how you want to live your retirement.

Your retirement plan

You may or may not have to make a decision right away. It is possible that your company may allow you to keep your money in the plan until you decide the best course to take.

However, if you have to make a choice between taking your retirement in a lump sum or receiving it in the form of a monthly annuity, choose the lump sum. It will give you a lot more flexibility. You will have the ability to take more (or less) income, or even to reach in and take a lump sum out in the event of an emergency. Or you can postpone taking anything out until you're 70½.

Getting your money

You have two choices here. First, you can have your employer pay you your retirement money directly. That would make it taxable plus carry a 10-percent penalty if you are under the age of 55. However, if you were born on or before January 1, 1936, you are eligible for five-year or 10-year averaging. That doesn't mean that you can pay the taxes over a longer period of time—it just gives you a reduced tax rate.

Your second choice is to transfer it into an IRA Rollover account. This allows you to defer the taxes until you remove the money. Don't worry if you are under the age of 55 and still need income. You can avoid the 10-percent early distribution penalty by doing "equal and substantial distributions." Review the previous chapter for a more detailed discussion.

Investing your retirement money

Even though you are retired, you still have need for growth on your money. Statistically, if you are married and you and your spouse are the same age, one of you will live to age 90. That's a long time. You need to invest a portion of your money with growth to keep up with inflation. Check my recommended allocation in Chapter 12 to see how to invest your money.

Also review Chapter 13 and determine how well you will be able to cope with your retirement. You will see if you have a need to continue to work in some form or fashion.

You must make the basic decision of whether you'd rather work with a financial advisor or go it alone. In either case, take advantage of no-load mutual funds. If you need help, find a fee-based financial planner who uses either no-load (preferably institutional) mutual funds or some form of professionally managed money. Remember, stockbrokers aren't usually good stock pickers.

Social Security

Now is the time to start preparing for Social Security. Review Chapter 8. Contact Social Security and see which month is best to claim benefits. It may be to your advantage to have your benefits begin in January, even if you don't plan on retiring until late in the year. Under current rules, many people can receive the most benefits possible with an application that is effective in January. Also, remember the special monthly rule that applies to your earnings for the first year of retirement.

Your home

If your home isn't paid for, work toward that objective. If you still have a substantial mortgage and your rate is 2 percent or more above the current rates, look into refinancing. Do it before you retire so you can meet the income qualifications. Call around to find the best rate in your area.

Credit cards

Use your credit cards for your convenience, not as a money-maker for the bank. Use them for car rentals. A Gold Card is especially good because of the insurance protection. Also you will need them to guarantee reservations at hotels. But don't carry a balance.

Cars

Buy two-year-old cars with a factory warranty. You don't need a new car from this point on. In fact, you never needed one. But now especially, take advantage of some of the good deals out there for used cars.

Outside investments

Your money should be invested pretty much like your retirement money: in line with your risk tolerance. However, you do have to consider taxes and the taxability of your Social Security.

You can reduce your taxes by using tax-advantaged mutual funds and tax-free bonds. You can reduce your current taxes and, depending on your income, the taxability of your Social Security by taking advantage of tax-deferred annuities.

College expenses

If you have kids in college, let them get a scholarship or borrow the money. There are plenty of plans available. Unless you're rolling in money, don't pay for it yourself with your retirement money. Don't mortgage your retirement for your children's education. I know this sounds selfish, but you do need to take care of yourself. Face it, no matter how great they may be, don't depend on them to support you during your retirement. They have their own lives to lead and their own families to raise.

Chapter 21

Bringing it all together: You can do it!

Well, we've reached the end of our journey. Now it's just a matter of putting all of this information to work.

Remember, retirement, like dieting, isn't easy, but it's simple. To lose weight, you have to eat the right foods and exercise. To gain financial security, you have to make smart spending decisions and invest your money wisely. In theory, neither of these is difficult. However in reality, they both can be tough—if you make them that way.

I've talked about having a vision, about focusing on the benefits of an action, and about making the proper choices. The right activity by you in these three areas will determine whether you become financially secure.

I am interested in the results you achieve from this book. Additionally, if you would like information on my personal investment services or my corporate preretirement seminars, you can reach me at:

Rosenberg Financial Group, Inc.
2517 Moody Rd., Suite 100
Warner Robins, GA 31088
(912) 922-8100 *or* (800) 777-0867

Good luck!

About the Author

Stephen M. Rosenberg, CFP, is an investment advisor and president of Rosenberg Financial Group. He is the author of a number of financial books, including *Keep Uncle Sam From Devouring Your Life Savings*, *Every Woman's Guide to Financial Security*, and *Last Minute Estate Planning*. He has appeared nationally as an expert on financial issues and teaches graduate courses for Mercer University in Macon, Ga. He serves as a featured speaker at pre-retirement seminars coast to coast and specializes in working with pre-retirees, retirees, and widows.

Index